CONCILIUM

CONCILIUM   2002/3

BRAZIL:
PEOPLE AND CHURCH(ES)

Edited by
José Oscar Beozzo and Luiz Carlos Susin

Translated from the Portuguese by
Paul Burns

SCM Press · London

Published by SCM Press, 9–17 St Albans Place, London N1 0NX

Copyright © Stichting Concilium

English translations copyright © 2002 SCM-Canterbury Press Ltd

ISBN 0 334 03067 6

Printed by Biddles Ltd, Guildford and King's Lynn

Concilium Published February, April, June, October
December

Contents

Introduction

JOSÉ OSCAR BEOZZO AND LUIZ CARLOS SUSIN

Contemporary Brazil is a living laboratory of expressions of faith and ancestral religions in new syntheses, flourishing in the winds of freedom blown by modernity. The foremost religious canon – virtually the only one that counts – is that of life experience and the encouragement of life in its basic dimensions: the body and its needs; the struggle for a livelihood; solidarity among neighbours; the symbolic expression of the sacred and the meanings it contains; the erotic, mystical, and playful dimensions of human existence.

The Brazilian 'condition' or 'history', like that of all parts of Latin America, began before 1500. That date officially marks the arrival of Portuguese navigators in lands that were to form what was later called Brazil. For at least 40,000 years, however, some 600 different peoples have been spreading over and taking root on this territory. Of those, 130 have survived extermination and the violent processes of integration. The majority, though, were thrown into the melting-pot of forced miscegenation with the Portuguese colonizers to which the native women were subjected. Some 4,000,000 Africans brought over as slaves were then added to the native peoples.

These native peoples and Africans have produced a mixed-race Brazil and endowed it with a strong cultural, religious, even ritual expression of the spiritual forces that rule life on earth and of indigenous contemplation and grace. The African slaves and their descendants have, through their resistance struggles, witnessed to the strength of life in adversity. They have kept deep ties with nature and with their ancestors, giving women a central position extending to their worship.

The economic and cultural history of Brazil is –officially – that of a colony of modern times, a colony facing first Europe and later also the United States. It was first a quarry for material extraction, then a dependent part of capitalist concentration of resources, and is now dependent on the concentration of technology and income, today on a globalized scale, which has been reproduced internally through a strongly vertical class hierarchy, the insignificance of the poor majority, and growing social exclusion and vio-lence.

In the interstices of official Catholicism, a popular Catholicism has developed, capable of nourishing resistance and dignity, self-esteem, and the sense of life, suffering, and death through a syncretic re-interpretation, with its own special traits coming from officially unrecognized sources, of indigenous and African traditions, despised but persistent and re-surfacing everywhere today. 'Lots of religion', 'Drink from every spring and refresh yourself in many ways to ward off danger' is a sacred command for the people of Brazil, something reflected in the best Brazilian literature, such as *Grande Sertão: Veredas*, by Guimarães Rosa.

On top of its original inhabitants and those transplanted by Portuguese colonization, Brazil has, from the mid-nineteenth century, received immi-grations from various countries of Europe and Asia, who have brought new Christian churches and new religions with them. Finally, globalization, in this part of the planet and as it affects religion, has poured the soup of tradi-tional Brazilian syntheses into a pot of Pentecostal and New Age stew, in a real 'carnival of the soul'.

The National Conference of Bishops of Brazil (CNBB) has been in exist-ence for fifty years. Founded by powerfully charismatic leaders such as Dom Hélder Câmara, it has had a strong presence on the Brazilian scene, filled with the spirit of the council and totally engaged in social questions. The Catholic Church has shown an energy and a creativity that have flowed into Brazilian society from the time of Catholic Action to engagement in organized social activities, such as trade unions and political parties. In the same way, pastoral strategy for land has produced what is the most organized and significant social and political movement of today, the Landless Workers Movement (MST). The rise of base church communities, further-more, is evidence of hope and prophecy within the church, of a participatory way of being church, of 'ecclesiogenesis', which, even if spread today over so many forms of popular church communities, organized in parishes and chapels, are still the true base on which the church rests.

In Brazil, various church denominations are flourishing, and Christian-ity's course is marked out by reasonably solid ecumenical frameworks, with official ecumenical bodies and innumerable partners in ecclesial and social initiatives affecting the whole of Brazilian society. The church's presence to the indigenous peoples and rural workers is likewise ecumenical in character.

The mega-cities, great state capitals such as São Paulo, Rio de Janeiro,

Belo Horizonte, and others, affected by grave risk of social disintegration and violence, have also become an arena for pastoral creativity, such as the 'dwellings' initiative for those who live and suffer on the streets, and similar initiatives for mothers and babies, street children, marginalized women, and the like.

The ecclesial face of Brazil is also marked by the conciliar form of religious life, which has taken the inspirations of the Medellín Conference to heart: the preferential option for the poor, 'insertion' in places where the bulk of the people live, accompanying the base communities. Among religious communities, those of women are outstanding for their missions in precarious situations, in 'priestless parishes', and in their social pastoral outreach, often putting their own lives at risk. The co-ordinating role of the Conference of Brazilian Religious has also been notable, running a number of services dedicated to the social and cultural 'insertion' of religious, besides being responsible for the maintenance and publications of a lively group of theologians.

In this social, ecclesial, and pastoral climate, the theology that sprang into life as liberation theology has also, in the last few years, taken on board the complexity of new soundings and of the emergence of new faces, voices, and subjects: feminists, blacks, economic, ecological, and ethical challenges. Theology has also widened its reach to include lay people, with people's courses, and at the same time has found a forum for governmental institutional recognition, thereby gaining a broad base and a more objective platform in the academic world.

The last few decades have, then, produced a real 'Brazilian ecclesiogenesis', which is still proceeding and which can be a valuable contribution to the world's churches. At the same time, it is facing a multiplicity of new situations that challenge pastoral action and theological reflection. The first of these is the globalization of problems and the world's loss of bearings, as part of the global crisis of Planet Earth: the crisis of rationality and the neo-paganism that have up to now affected mainly the First World; the crisis of insignificance, which has prolonged poverty and whose first victim has been Latin America; the crisis of cultural pluralism, which has affected colonial and post-colonial Africa; the crisis of religious pluralism, whose cradle was in Asia – all these have now become a complex and world-wide crisis under the impact of market-driven globalization, leaving everyone on the entire planet bereft of a sure and peaceful course. In Brazil, the intense growth of Pentecostalism, including the special case of Catholic Charismatic Renewal, and the ingenuity shown by religions in accepting New Age concepts, are attempts – sometimes courageous ones, sometimes exasperated, sometimes ambiguous – to respond to this situation.

In ecclesial terms, nonetheless, the greatest challenges – even giving this word a positive sense – appear to come from the ever more prominent place occupied by women in the churches: with energy and application, they are ministering to the people, leading pastoral endeavours, facing up to conflicts arising from the traditional hierarchy of power. There is also the bubbling-up of creative thought coming from Afro-Brazilians and the black movements, not to mention a challenge that has not yet been sufficiently appreciated: that of the relevance or otherwise of evangelization campaigns carried out through the more complex aspects of culture, especially formal education, university courses, and the communications media. Inevitably, a large part of the church's resources is concentrated on education.

Finally, faced with a nation in which, under the cloak of freedom and globalization of the market, the state is reducing its own scope and reducing the public sector and social services, while at the same time carrying out privatizations that mean transnationalization, unemployment, an increase in poverty and in the informal sector of the economy, a growing incidence of corruption and violence at all levels, what is possible for a church when ethics, justice, and life for all become the imperatives deriving from the people themselves?

Brazil shares the problems, strengths, and hopes of the majority of Latin American countries and of those of most regions of the world. It is not unique. That is why the 'news' that follows may possibly prove to be a help in bringing peoples suffering their birth pangs closer together.

I. The Human Condition

The Formation of the Brazilian People

LUIZ EDUARDO W. WANDERLEY

'Formation' involves an explanation of the people, the nation, and the state. We are a people marked by a multiplicity of ethnic groups, cultures, and languages. We have been dependent on foreign countries from the sixteenth century to the present time. We have the eighth largest economy in the world and are one of the most unequal societies on the planet, besides having huge disparities between one region and another. Our population is both cordial and violent. I shall proceed to a brief account of how it came to be.

At the outset, the Europeans were confronted with strangers, the indigenous people. They provided a different view of the world, a different identity, different costumes, myths, stories, traditions. In the opinion of the Peruvian Quijano, one phase of modernity began back then in the sixteenth century, since the Europeans had to change their conceptions of history and life. Roman theology pondered whether the Indians had souls. Five hundred years later we are still debating whether there was a 'discovery' or an encounter, since various tribes had lived there for ages.

The Portuguese colonizers came from the lower classes and brought the myth of paradise lost, of an idyllic land filled with riches. Their aims, mainly economic and commercial, involved both political and religious spheres. Our first face emerged from the encounter between Portuguese and indigenous. Colonization brought our first dependence on the outside world, in administration and commerce (hardwoods, sugar). The first miscegenation came about. Missionary catechesis was linked to imperial aims: Portuguese-ization equalled evangelization! Conquest of land and of minds continued: for centuries, religious alone could teach. The results were genocide, slavery, and the attempt to eradicate the religion of the indigenous peoples. Some missionaries were critical of these procedures, and the Jesuit 'missions' sought to control their people while offering them a worthy life – some have spoken of these 'reductions' as the first essay in communism in the world. For decades, the Indians resisted, and they are still with us today: the thousands that survive (estimates say some 300,000) struggle against ranchers and miners, defend the demarcation of their territory, seek a bilingual education. Some victories have been won over the years: the Indian Protection Service, 1910; the National Foundation for the Indian, 1968; the Indian Statute, making the state responsible for protecting them. An important role has been played by the Indigenist Missionary Council (CIMI, 1972), linked to the Catholic Church, which seeks to protect them and to bring about an inculturation, despite disputes with some anthropologists.

Then came the blacks, torn from their native lands, ushering in a new, harsh, and terrible slavery. Blacks were considered merchandise, not persons. There was a further process of miscegenation in the great houses and on plantations. This led to memorable struggles, flights, and creation of black communities, *Quilombos*, many of which were terribly destroyed (as in the case of Palmares in the eighteenth century). Between the sixteenth and the mid-nineteenth centuries we took some four million blacks, and we were the last country to abolish slavery, which we did without creating adequate conditions for integrating blacks into society. Some people see the formation of our so-called racial democracy as a positive factor (apparently our discrimination is not as deep as that in the United States, for example), but others regard it as a myth, since white prejudice against blacks persists in the collective unconscious and in daily practice – with a wide disparity in earnings and educational opportunities between white and black, and the tendency of the police to regard blacks as potential criminals, for example. More fundamentalist political sectors have continued to defend racism in favour of the whites. Black people's influence is to be found in their cultural and religious roots and in the colour of the populace: in music, food, dance, Afro-Brazilian religions, costumes, languages. There is the paradox of skin colour, with some people trying to lighten theirs, or to identify themselves as brown, mulatto, or mameluke, while the body that carries out national censuses (Brazilian Institute of Geography and Statistics) has for a long time not included colour among its questions. Others maintain the greatness of their ethnic origin and are proud to be classed as black: hence the formation of numerous movements and groups, political and other, made up of black people campaigning for their race, their role in Brazilian history, their effective emancipation – still not fully achieved today.

Women, besides the sexual miscegenation forced on Indians and blacks 'to populate the land', have always had to contend with domination by the man in the patriarchal family. For centuries, they have been subjected to violence in the home and the workplace, and despite the gradual advances they have made, they still suffer subordination and exploitation. While in the past their resistance was on the local and above all the individual level, in the last few decades they have organized themselves into Councils and Delegations to defend their interests. Today women make up a growing proportion of the workforce and are becoming quite prominent on the political scene. (In this context it is worth recalling the claims made on behalf of natives, blacks, and women at the Durban Meeting in South Africa in September 2001, demanding a gesture of repentance from the colonial powers and even financial compensation for the historical wrongs they had suffered.)

Following the black influx, we had the arrival of the first wave of immigrants from Europe and elsewhere in the late nineteenth and early twentieth centuries: Italians, Germans, Poles, Syrio-Lebanese, Japanese, fleeing from persecutions or other perils in their own countries. They came to take the place of slave labour and worked in agriculture, trade, and the beginnings of industrialization. They were faced with harsh conditions and were refused citizenship. The earliest workers' revolts in the country were supported by some of these immigrants (the anarcho-syndicalists of São Paulo). Many of the Germans and Japanese were persecuted during the Second World War. Taken as a whole, they have played an active part and exerted a decisive influence in the formation of the Brazilian nationality, whether through contributing to development as workers or owners (some became wealthy and prominent figures in the rural, industrial, commercial, banking, and financial worlds), or through blending their costumes, clothes, traditions, thoughts, religions, manners of seeing and acting with those of the Brazilians already installed here. A second wave brought immigrants from other countries such as Korea, Bolivia, and Paraguay, nearly all illegal and working in the black economy but equally seeking to integrate their ways of thinking and acting with those of Brazilians.

Another major factor has been internal migration, brought about mainly by the growth of capitalism in the south-east and south of the country and by the move away from the countryside, attracting waves of migrants from the rural areas to the cities and from less developed to more developed regions.

These migrants have also had a specially marked effect on the culture, work, and leisure of the areas in which they have settled. The construction of the new capital, Brasilia, by migrant workers has been a significant case. Their presence at various periods has brought and is still bringing contrasts: we still regard certain groups as strangers, accusing them of keeping to less than truly capitalist attitudes and behaviour (through sticking to country habits still not contaminated with urban ways typical of capitalism), while we value other groups for their effective contribution to development and for the regional culture they represent, which is seen as enriching the national repertoire.

The historical importance of peasants and rural labourers as a group makes it essential to mention them. From the early days of colonization to the present, these country people have made an essential contribution to feeding the population and enriching exporters. Subjugated by country landowners and by laws for decades (they were forbidden to buy land and prevented from voting), living under harsh conditions, they also set up resistance movements (from the mute protest of migration to organized – and brutally repressed – struggles, such as those in Canudos in Bahia in 1887 and Contestado in Santa Catarina in 1916, in which the religious element was a basic part of their identity and motivation). More recently, better laws have been passed, such as the Rural Workers Statutes of 1963, and movements such as the Country Leagues and rural trade unions have developed since the 1950s and 1960s. Today, with the Union Centre (National Confederation of Workers in Agriculture) and the Landless Workers Movement, this contingent of the population has a powerful presence of the national scene, despite the increased pace of urbanization in recent times. The influence of country people on all sectors of national life, expressed in culture, in religion, in diet, in political life and other areas has been constant throughout our history and is still strong.

Over the whole of the workforce, the conditions current in the early period of industrialization showed the same abuses as found in Europe. The working day was between eight and fourteen hours, the disciplinary regime was draconian, and there were generally no labour contracts, holidays, or weekends. Before 1917 the 'labour question' was hardly raised, and when it became more serious it was regarded as a 'police matter'. Repression of the workers was brutal, and it was not until the mid-twentieth century that progressive labour legislation was brought in (based on the Italian model). But there was a large gap between the letter of the law and its application, and workers had to struggle tirelessly, mainly through their trade unions, to ensure compliance and to win new concessions. During the period of the military dictatorship (mid 1960s to 1980s) they were kept severely in check but gradually progressed through so-called 'combative base unionism', followed by the creation of 'sector chambers', to make agreements between employers, employees, and sometimes the government, and new 'union centres' (in particular the 'workers' central' and 'union power'). In recent years, faced with changes in the social division of labour brought about by globalization and free-market economics (privatizations, the diminished role of the state in social policy, temporary work, structural unemployment, the black economy), the workers' overall situation has become more precarious, and new forms of resistance and struggle are being devised.

Our political and economic élites and the ruling classes deserve special mention. These élites have held power and control in the country for five hundred years, sometimes embodying ideas and practices brought from overseas and even allying themselves to foreign élites, sometimes trying to uphold certain national characteristics. A significant number of their children have studied in Europe, though more now go to the US, while still keeping their ties to the Old World. Considerable numbers among these élites hold conservative and reactionary views, are dazzled by the so-called First World and with the theories proceeding from the wealthy nations – in the recent past concepts of development and now free-market ideology and the measures proposed by the World Bank, the IMF, the WTO, and the Washington Accord – and keep their money in foreign banks (in strong-currency zones and tax havens). They have always feared communism and been ready to declare states of emergency. Allied to equally conservative and reactionary sectors of the armed forces, they react to any fairly organized left-wing opposition by pressing for authoritarian regimes and military power. They travel frequently and live a high-consumption lifestyle, residing in palaces or imposing mansions, keeping up with the latest fashions, driving luxury cars, using the best schools and universities, eating in the smartest restaurants. They see poverty as natural and have lately become concerned with the growth in violence. Small groups with links to large businesses and banks have set up philanthropic Foundations to attend to excluded sectors of the population, establishing fairly far-reaching programmes, which have become known as the Third Sector.

One problem addressed by thinkers, academics, social scientists, and intellectuals is how to overcome the still widespread backwardness in society, particularly in rural areas, basically on medium-sized and large tracts of privately-owned land (today large corporations have joined the land-owning classes), where landowners prevent the implementation of basic agrarian reforms capable of remedying the wretched plight of small-holders and the landless. Those who defend this backwardness (in culture and politics) make allies out of others who seek to uphold the existing class system and block potentially radical proposals such as changes in the tax system, political reform and other wide-reaching social ideas. The mass communications media are in general organically bound to the power-holders and de-politicize the masses.

Society and the state in Brazil both have features that adversely affect the implementation of a true democracy: authoritarianism, 'physiologism', paternalism, and so on. Promising steps have been taken towards democra-tizing political institutions, but very few in the direction of economic or social democracy. Valiant efforts have been made on the local level. The Catholic Church, despite the historical alliance between its hierarchy and the élites and ruling classes, has played an important part in philanthropy and social aid programmes, and since the mid-twentieth century has con-sistently taken an actively critical approach, denouncing injustices and the capitalist system and preaching reforms, besides encouraging progressive movements and groups. Secular society has also become more aware and better organized, thereby strengthening the public arena.

The following works (in Portuguese) by major historians and social sciences can serve as a basis for further reading: Sérgio Buarque de Holanda, *Raízes do Brasil*; Caio Prado Junior *História Econômica do Brasil*; Paulo Prado, *Retrato do Brasil*; Gilberto Freyre, *Casa-grande & Senzala*; Raymundo Faoro, *Os donos do poder*; Frei Vicente do Salvador, *História da Custódia do Brasil*; Fernando Novais, *Portugal e o Brasil na crise do antigo sistema colonial*; Euclydes da Cunha, *Os sertões*; Serafim Leite, *História da Companhia de Jesus no Brasil*; Capistrano de Abreu, *O descobrimento do Brasil*; Francisco A. Varnhagen, *História Geral do Brasil*; Emília Viotti da Costa, *Da senzala à colônia*; Darcy Ribeiro, *A formação do povo brasileiro*; Antônio Cândido, *Formação da literatura brasileira*; Boris Fausto, *História do Brasil*; José Honório Rodrigues, *Conciliação e reforma no Brasil*; Florestan Fernandes, *A revolução burguesa no Brasil*; Oliveira Viana, *Instituições políticas brasileiras*; Alfredo Bosi, *Dialética da colonização*; Luís da Câmara Cascudo, *Antologia do folclore brasileiro*; Octávio Ianni, *Raças e classes no Brasil*; José de Souza Martins, *Capitalismo e tradicionalismo*; Marilena Chauí, *O mito fundador do Brasil.*

New Age: An Errant Religious Culture in Brazil Today

LEILA AMARAL

In general, the term New Age can be taken as referring to a spiritual phenomenon that has been spreading through the world of today since the 1960s, beginning to affect Brazil in the 1970s. A number of currents come together in it: (a) that of the inheritors of counter-culture, with its ideas for alternative communities; (b) that of self-fulfillment, based on therapeutic concepts drawing on mystical experiences and holistic philosophies and relating them to modern scientific theories; (c) those drawn to the occult, basing themselves on the esoteric movements of the nineteenth century and encounters with Eastern, folk and indigenous religions; (d) the ecological discourse of sacralization of nature and of the cosmic encounter of the self with its essence and inner perfection; and (e) the 'yuppie'reinterpretation of that spirituality focussed on inner perfection through 'new age'services for personnel training offered to the human resources' departments of capitalist enterprises.

Besides this general definition, I use the term New Age to suggest a more theoretical concept, one capable of embracing what I consider specific to an 'errant religious culture' at this dawn of a new century: the possibility of certain spiritual and religious experiences changing, stylizing, disarranging or rearranging elements of previously existing traditions and making these elements into metaphors for systematically evoking particular sensations or visions, to make particular instances stand out and according to particular objectives.

I. Urban 'holistic centres' and their kaleidoscopic religiosity

In Brazil the spiritual outreach of New Age is greatest in the cities, through the various services offered by 'holistic centres', which provide activities bringing together an extensive and varied network of services, such as:

alternative therapies; Eastern-inspired exercises; shamanist experiences; workshops and courses on philosophical and religious beliefs and principles from a variety of cultural sources; not to mention products such as religious and self-help books and CDs, crystals, incense, images of angels and demons, and so on. These holistic centres – of which the anthropologist José Guilherme Magnani has counted some 842 in the city of São Paulo alone[1] – do not restrict themselves to one basic activity or attach themselves to any dogmatic system; they have no closed body of teaching or rites of initiation, and they concentrate not on merely selling products but on events known, in Brazil, as 'workshops'. They put themselves forward as special places for providing services and carrying out specific and immediate actions, with a spiritual purpose that may be therapeutic, artistic or playful, depending on the individual needs of people, who build up a sort of religious experience through the mutual interpenetration of various spiritual and non-spiritual fields.

They do all they can to provide a pleasant setting, creating an atmosphere of leisure and culture. Their clients, whose numbers are fairly steady, are drawn to them by the style of life they offer and by sharing in collective 'experiences', *but nevertheless without forming a traditional type of religious community or cult.* This leisured, cultured atmosphere contributes to *an uneven frequentation*, due to the variety of different and original events from which to choose from among the wide spread of alternatives offered by the city. The programmes also provide a sort of *global communication network* linking holistic centres, ashrams and New Age alternative communities, extending beyond national boundaries.

In Brazil, since the second half of the 1980s, the emphasis on New Age theories and practices has increasingly been on the therapeutic aspect,[2] and on the contribution these therapies can make to 'personal development' through what is known as 'therapeutic spirituality'. Unlike specifically 'religious' therapeutic practices, however, this spirituality does not necessarily refer to any single religious cosmology.[3]

'Workshop' is the term most widely used to describe these therapeutic-spiritual experiences. They are means offered to individuals or groups not so much in order to provide doctrinal messages or codes by which to change their lives as in order to give them, by 'practical means', a sort of emotional stimulus that can encourage them to set free their 'full life potential'. They are driven by a desire for change, in harmony with the 'creative forces' of the universe as 'prevailing powers'. Starting from the basic menu, many other 'workshops' can be provided through extensive combinations of their various elements and incorporation of other artistic, mythical and ritual constructs available in the market place of religious and cultural goods. The whole phenomenon is a heterogenous one, with its great variety extending over the *social profile of its frequenters*. Within this, the phenomenon gains most of its adherents from among the middle and upper classes.

According to research carried out by Martins in Recife, 72.4% of those interviewed have completed tertiary education. Of these, most call themselves Catholic (41% of the total). Adding the 'spiritist' followers of Kardec,[4] this figure rises to nearly 57%. Significantly, 24.1% of the sample say they have no religion. By occupation, most respondents work in the liberal professions; in answer to 'Reasons for choosing alternative therapies', emphasis is placed on existential (27.6%), spiritual (21.2%) or emotional (19.1%) ones. The question of physical sicknesses, though significant (12.7%), is consistently secondary compared to the above aspects.[5]

Turning to the various levels of manner of belonging, working-out and elaboration of the basis of the practices devotees follow, I make use of the typology established by Magnani in his research in the city of São Paulo.[6]

- Erudite type: made up of professionals with greater understanding and knowledge of the subject they specialize in. They differ from the participative type in that their choices are limited and little inclined to heterodox combinations. They normally relate to a single religious, philosophical or therapeutic matrix, or, if they make their own combination, they tend to present this as forming a coherent whole.
- Participative type: the typical frequenters and leading consumers of the products and events on offer. Their choices and combinations are made on the basis of information they seek to derive on the themes and codes that underly the offerings, from within this heterogenous universe. Unlike the 'erudite', they do not regulate their actions in accordance with just one of the religious, therapeutic and philosophical systems. On the contrary, they move freely from one to another, trying out, without problems, activities and practices derived from all the diffewrent systems.
- Occasional type: made up of those who frequent and take part in events in a non-systematic way and are attracted more by the 'market' appeal than by knowledge of or familiarity with the codes available.[7]

It is the participative type who form the main target audience for the lectures, courses and workshops offered by the holistic centres. I would add that it is also from this category of adherents that many of the present 'facilitators' and 'focussers' of New Age workshops are drawn, rather than from among the 'erudite'. They include artists, writers, therapists, teachers, sociologists, anthropologists and psychologists who, besides attending the various lectures, courses and workshops provided by the erudite, build up a 'spiritual-therapeutic capital' by travelling over the vast area of Brazil and visiting other continents. They develop the particular, personal experiences thus gained to create ever new combinations based on elements lifted from the different traditions they have visited, which are in turn incorporated into hypotheses related to scientific discussions of subjects such quantum physics, psychology, and anthropology.

Combining one thing with another with such ease, they are capable of offering a simultaneous experience of artistic, spiritual and therapeutic styles that need not be simultaneous in either space or time. Besides, what confers legitimacy on this combinatory activity is just this capacity the 'facilitators' have for evoking in the experiences they offer – either by simulation or by representation – what are seen as 'creative forces' coming from other ages, other places and other cultures; that is, for enabling these 'forces' to pass across time and space.

So by the phrase 'kaleidoscopic religiosity' I am not referring just to the practices of individual participants, of those who undertake a journey with no fixed goal among the different religious or therapeutic-spiritual offerings, making their own combinations and individual syntheses. What I mean in the first place is the dynamic inherent in the make-up of the experiences on offer: the disjunction of hybrid differences in a constant process of re-combination, whose originality is the very radicalness of its currency.

II. The hegemony of the shamanist model

Techniques used to attain the above objectives include 'creative visualization' or 'shamanic journeys' used in combination with technique of physical stimulation.

'Healing', according to this model, means 'journeying' to the non-material realm. Using creative visualization, the shaman, who may be either the patient or the healer, seeks to penetrate as deeply as possible into the material realm (within his own body), to the point where he feels himself to be *like waves of energy or waves of possibility*, a world made up of elementary particles that are nothing other than tendencies to exist. This non-material substrate, drawn from the quantum metaphor, is interpreted by the New Age outlook as 'pure idea' or 'primal energy'. The idea of a solid world is pushed into the background, so as to bring forward the concept of process, of a completely changeable and expanding world, and of healing as 'constant transformation', which can affect both individuals and the wider environment.

'Workshops' in this scenario become a regulated process leading those who take part in them into experience of life's drama and into their own process of change. Being 'spiritual' or 'primal' means in effect acquiring the quality of 'ongoing change', the objectives of which are: (a) understanding of one's own potentialities, metaphorically related to the 'animal power' of each of the participants; (b) correction of one's inner imbalances, particularly fear of living life.

The metaphor and the use of shamanic symbols are borrowed from indigenous societies that practise shamanism, but this does not produce a variant of shamanism as understood by anthropologists within the sociological and cosmological context of each group studied. In New Age circles, the shamanism of indigenous societies is used as a metaphor for speaking, through 'workshops', about existence and the possibility of moving between two worlds at the same time: the physical world – the world of one's culture, society, or tribe – and the spiritual world – the world of one's spirits and ancestors, which in the New Age universe metaphorically represent the flight of consciousness beyond the limits of a single civilization, culture, or society.

For primitive peoples consciousness, like spirits, flies. Consciousness flies to the savage world of the mind, still not totally domesticated by society, just as spirits in primitive societies fly to the world of the ancestors. Consciousness flies, removes itself to an 'imaginal' reality, to a mental state in which any transformation can come about. In this way creative visualizations work to enable the participants to attain, systematically, consciousness of this movement of the spirit, in which individuals affirm themselves as spirits in movement, through an arrangement of constructed techniques, ' "by means of assembling elements from a great variety of sources, cultural contexts and historical periods" . . . The sources that furnish the inspiration, doctrinal base and ritual elements are fairly diverse: they run from works by revered writers such as Mircéa Eliade, Joseph Campbell and Carl Gustav Jung, among others, through traditions and cosmologies attributed to indigenous peoples (present and past), to pre-historical cultures and now vanished religions, and in some cases they go so far as to include formulations from particular sciences such as molecular biology, genetics, and quantum physics.'[8]

III. Indigenization: a typically Brazilian version of New Age?

Thanks to the growing influence of the shamanic model in New Age spiritual circles, shamanic experiences are also being offered by the holistic centres in Brazilian cities. Experiences on offer incorporate mythic and ritual elements taken from various shamanic traditions of the indigenous peoples of Brazil, with an admixture of those of Native American tribes from North America and the Andean cultures and pre-Buddhist Tibetan traditions from central and northern Asia.

The New Age environment does not, however, require the shamans or facilitators of a shamanic experience to come from indigenous tribes. Very often they do not. Through courses run in Brazil, as well as a transnational shamanic network offering instruction and initiation in the most varied shamanic practices, or a combination of the two, Brazilians from all ethnic groups can call themselves shamans and offer their particualar recipes. Some of these urban shamans, following the example of Carlos Castañeda, end by 'converting' after contact with indigenous Brazilian cultures through academic research into them and, after a period of initiation with the natives, move on to offer their services in the big cities. Other shamans, who claim to be descended from indigenous groups, re-work and build on elements taken generically from Brazilian Indian traditions mixed with elements from other traditions. Others, such as the shaman Sapaim, whose indigenous origin is proven, offer consultations in the cities to non-Indian clients, cultured men and women who have university degrees but who understand little or nothing of the magic words pronounced by Sapaim in *tupi kamaiurá*. According to Wesley Aragão, clients recreate the shaman from within their own worlds.[9] It is worth emphasizing that, despite the presence of references to different sources and traditions on both the discursive level and that of basic decision-making that make up a workshop, in practice what predominates is an intense shift between them, between vestiges of their rituals and their myths, besides the linking of shamanic experiences, so constituted, with other very different areas of spiritual, therapeutic, artistic, and scientific procedures.

Following this same logic and the vein opened by the influence of neo-shamanism in New Age circles, there is considerable evidence of the use of the hallucinogen *ayahuasca* to promote altered states of consciousness, stemming from incorporation of ritual elements borrowed from religions of Daime.[10] This is used for therapeutic and artistic-creative purposes by segments of the middle classes of south-eastern Brazil, following various strands of hallucinogenic traditions. Outside holistic centres, shamanic workshops, combined with Daimist use of *ayahuasca*, Western psychotherapies, and spiritual traditions from all parts of the globe, have also spread to medical clinics, mainly psychotherapeutic ones, to provide their patients with rapid access to their unconscious dimension.[11]

In short, 'a homeless spirit'.

Notes

1. J. G. C. Magnani, 'O circuito neo-esotérico na cidade de São Paulo', in M. J. Carozzi (ed.), *A Nova Era no Mercosul*, Petrópolis 1999, pp.27–8.

2. See F. Tavares, 'Alquimias da Cura: um estudo sobre a rede terapêutica alternativa no Rio de Janeiro' (doctoral thesis, Rio de Janeiro: UFRJ/PPGS/IFCS, 1998). Tavares lists 199 forms of alternative therapies, compared to 31 conventional, divided into the following categories: alternative medical practices (3), which include homeopathy, for example; bodily therapies (5); techniques of treatment and diagnosis (118), subdivided into 17 subtopics – acupuncture, organic food, astrology, chakras, crystals, colours, Kirlian effect, florals, rainbow, massage, pendulum, psychotherapy, shiatsu, breathing, past lives, visualization, Yoga, and others; massage (18); practicals and workshops (55), subdivided into 13 subtopics – diet, arts, martial arts, bodily awareness, dances, maternity, posture, psycho-production, relaxation, breathing, Yoga and others; aesthetics (5).

3. Tavares, 'O holismo terapêutico no âmbito do movimento Nova Era no Rio de Janeiro', in Carozzi, op.cit.

4. Born Hippolyte Léon Deuizard in France in 1804, he took the name Allan Kardec from a 'spirit protector' who told him this had been his name in a previous incarnation. His *Book of Spirits* was published in 1857 and *Book of Mediums* in 1861. He died in 1869. His following is greatest in Brazil (where his books are still printed in millions on presses owned by a prominent Catholic publishing house, which regards him as basically 'on the side of life'), but has followers also in France, Spain, Germany, Australia and elsewhere (trans.).

5. P. H. Martins, 'As Terapias Alternativas e a Libertação dos Corpos', in Carozzi, op. cit.

6. Magnani, *Mystica Urbe: um estudo antroplológico sobre o circuito neo-esotérico na metrópole*, São Paulo 1999.

7. Magnani, op. cit.

8. Magnani, 'O xamanismo urbano e a religiosidade contemporânea' in: *Religião e Sociedade*, vol.20, no.2 (1999), p.118.

9. The existence of this type of shaman came to my notice through the doctoral thesis by Wesley Aragão, 'Os xamãs na metrópole e a busca pela sabedoria do Bom Selvagem' (Rio de Janeiro, UFRJ).

10. The Teaching of 'Saint Daime' belongs to the Brazilian part of the Amazon basin. It consists of a complex ritual based on consumption of *ayahuasca*, a hallucinogenic drink made from mixing *jagube* juice with *chacrona* leaves, long known to the Indians native to the region before being extended to settlers during the migrations of the 1930s. The teaching is a syncretic combination of different religious traditions such as Kardec's Spiritism, Afro-Brazilian religions and popular Catholicism. Since the 1980s middle-class people from the south and south-east of Brazil have been attracted by the Teaching of Saint Daime, forming communities in these regions of the country or joining the Céu do Mapiá community in Acre, from where the spiritual and social model behind the Teaching comes. See L. Amaral, *Carnaval da Alma: Comunidade, Essência e Sincretismo na Nova Era*, Petrópolis 2000.

11. See Beatriz Labate, *A Reinvenção do Uso da Ayahausca nos Centros Urbanos* (master's dissertration in social anthropology, UNICAMP, 2000).

II. Forms of Church Presence and Activities

Fifty Years of the CNBB: A Bishops' Conference Based on the Council:

Evangelization Projects; Political and Ecclesiastical Tensions and Challenges

CARDINAL ALOÍSIO LORSCHEIDER

I. Historical facts and statistics

The National Bishops' Conference of Brazil (CNBB) was largely the personal inspiration of Dom Hélder Pessoa Câmara. It was founded in October 1952, in Rio de Janeiro. At that time, Dom Hélder was auxiliary archbishop of Rio.

To speak of the Conference today is to speak of the whole Brazilian church. The Conference has carried out – and is still carrying out today – the evangelization process stemming from Vatican II, from Medellín, Puebla, and Santo Domingo, from world synods of bishops and from the Synod of America. The voice of the Conference is the voice of the church in Brazil.

There are at present 420 bishops in Brazil, of whom 110 are *emeriti*.

1. Pastoral planning

Its pastoral planning has characterized all the Conference's evangelizing activity. The more organized planning strategy began in April 1962, primarily with an *Emergency Plan* for the church, followed by a *Five-year Plan* (1966–70); then from 1971 there were General Directives for pastoral-evangelizing action and biennial plans drawn up by the Conference's general secretary, involving reviews of the national plan.

2. The Emergency Plan

This marked the beginning of systematic planning by the CNBB. The plan was published in April 1962. It contained excellent preparation by the Brazilian bishops for Vatican II. The plan's basic concern was to form communities of faith, worship, and charity within the scheme of Jesus' triple office: prophetic, priestly, kingly. For the first time, it envisaged an overall pastoral strategy.

At the time the bishops felt the lack of objective data on the true situation as a key deficiency.

3. The Five-year Plan (1966–70)

Once the council had ended, the bishops launched a Five-year Plan. The intention of this was to create favourable conditions and measures to adjust the Brazilian church as quickly and as fully as possible to the vision of Vatican II. *Six lines*, later called *six dimensions*, were worked out as reference points for all evangelizing pastoral action. They formed a sort of synthesis of Vatican II in the minds of the bishops. The lines were: visible unity, missionary action, catechetical action, ecumenical action (later broadened to include inter-religious dialogue), and building a world according to God's plan.

The actual plan contained ongoing activities, development of some services, special activities, and establishment of new services.

When they reviewed the plan in 1970, the bishops decided that they would no longer have a national plan but just national directives, with biennial plans for the national bodies of the CNBB. Up to the present, fifteen biennial plans have been prepared for the national bodies, and every four years, after a review of these, the Conference holds a General Assembly to review the general directives for the whole of Brazil.

4. The 'Toward the New Millennium' and 'Looking ahead' projects

To prepare for the Jubilee Year of 2000, the CNBB published an evangelization project divided into four years: of these, 1997 focussed on the person of Jesus Christ, faith, and baptism, using Mark's Gospel as a backcloth; 1998 concentrated on the person of the Holy Spirit, hope, and confirmation, following Luke's Gospel; 1999 studied the person of God the Father, charity, and reconciliation, using the Gospel according to Matthew; finally, the subject matter for 2000 was the glorification of the Holy Trinity, with special attention to the eucharist, the celebration of the Jubilee, and five hundred years of evangelization in Brazil, using the Gospel of John as a study text.

In this project all the evangelization was ordered on the basis of four evangelizing requirements: *witness, service, dialogue, proclamation.* Without abandoning the six dimensions of pastoral action, a process was begun to emphasize these four requirements, which became the reference points for an increasingly incarnate and inculturated evangelization.

Once the Jubilee of 2000 was over, the CNBB launched a new project, *Being Church in the New Millennium,* with the aim of renewing understanding of the identity and mission of the church in Brazil. Looking at the situation of the world today, there is cause for possible discouragement. However, pessimism cannot be allowed to overtake us. We have to look forward. If it is a fact that we are tired today, it is equally a fact that there will be a harvest tomorrow. What we sow today, we shall indubitably reap tomorrow. We have to persevere in the clear and ineluctable proclamation of Jesus in the whole of his mystery, which is prolonged in time and space by the church. The New Testament book that inspires this CNBB project is the Acts of the Apostles.

5. The Brotherhood Campaign

This is a campaign that the CNBB has carried out in Lent since 1964. It begins on Ash Wednesday and ends on Palm Sunday.

It is an extraordinary and massive demonstration of evangelization. The church marks this period with its presence in the social commuication media, in schools, in catechesis, and in the liturgy. Each year special resources are allocated to reflection, chants, celebrations, and slogans. Some years back, the campaign was opened with a discourse from the Pope, transmitted by all the media.

The subjects dealt with by the campaign over its thirty-eight years can be divided into three phases:

1. search for internal renewal of the church, from 1964 to 1972;
2. the social situation of the people, denouncing social sin and promoting justice, lasting from 1973 to 1984;
3. existential situations of the Brazilian people, from 1985 to the present. The 2002 campaign focussed on the indigenous peoples.

The Brotherhood campaign is a very powerful demonstration of church unity in Brazil. It asks everyone who takes part to make a specific gesture as a Lenten penance, related to the subject and spirit of the campaign.

II. Problems, challenges, tensions

There are many problems and challenges: the just use and ownership of land; immigration pastoral policy; the formation and encouragement of base church communities; pastoral policy for the cities, for Amazonia, for families, for vocations, for young people; defence and promotion of human rights, with especial attention to the question of indigenous peoples and Afro-Brazilians; the balance between faith and life, taking account of popular piety or the people's religion, which has been a major element in Brazil; the problem of the various religious movements outside the Catholic Church.

The great step that the church in Brazil has begun to take, through the actions of the CNBB, is the *shift in its social setting*. This means moving from being a church more linked to the upper and middle classes to being a church of the people, within a process of increased participation and communion, in which all can have a voice and a place, feeling themselves to be church, in a liberating atmosphere of free persons, not dominated, not oppressed, not marginalized, excluded, or pushed aside.

The viewpoint of the poor is increasingly inspiring the evangelizing action taken by the church in Brazil.

As for the *tensions*, these arise not so much in the *doctrinal* field but far more out of the *life situation* of our people. The reason the Conference is attacked, calumniated, misunderstood, is nearly always its *social policy*. It is accused of putting the *spiritual or religious and eternal* side of life to one side, of acting almost like a trade union, looking after the interests of just one class, the poor.

Making a strict list of the subjects tackled by the Conference in its annual Plenary Assemblies and studying the whole collection of its studies and documents would show that the number of strictly religious subjects, of matters relating to the inner life of the church, is far greater than that of questions relating to the social order. The fact of the matter is that questions of social order are of greater interest to the media, and this can give a distorted view of the evangelizing work of the Conference. What troubles some people is that the church tries to carry out its evangelization *starting from the poor*. This approach is interpreted as though it meant an *exclusive or excluding* option. The *preferential* option for the poor is read as though it were a preference *only* for the poor. It ceases to be preferential and becomes partisan. And then it is caught up in the class struggle. If such were the case, this option would cease to be evangelical and prophetic but would become a-political, though tinged with party politics.

There is no denying that some church people may have gone too far in one direction, but this cannot be said of the Conference, to the extent that it speaks and acts in the name of the Brazilian church. The role of the church is *social-critical-prophetic*. We always have to keep the balance within the incarnation of the Word, which is the taking on of all that is human in an indissoluble union, without confusion or dilution, with what is divine in the Person of the Word. In the real world, this means a constant search for true and actual harmony between faith and life: not only individual sin or only social sin; not only orthopraxis; not only the spiritual dimension; not only the social and political dimension; not only inner conversion; not only change of structures.

III. Results achieved

One of the very positive results has been that the church in Brazil, without sidelining the people's religion or popular piety, has managed to make the people's faith more conscious and lively. This shows in liturgical celebrations, in a liturgy that is, without any doubt, a celebration of the mysteries of our faith but is also a celebration of the particular mysteries of people's lives. Celebration takes on the simultaneous qualities of *kerygma*, evangelization, catechesis, liturgy.

Another very positive result has been that pastoral planning has helped us to experience the collegiality of bishops in a positive fashion.

There has also been an increased integration of the church with the mission territories, with a growing missionary commitment overseas, particularly in relation to Africa.

The church has gained greater independence from the state. The difficulties faced during the 'regime of exception' from 1964 to 1985 helped to bring this about. The bishops and clergy have at the same time drawn closer to the people. The church has become more disciple than teacher. The church has set itself to *listen to the people*. It has had a rich experience of the *sensus fidelium*.

There has also been development of a theology of services, ministries, and charisms.

Ecumenical and inter-religious dialogue has intensified, despite the reservations of some Christian groups and others averse to any type of dialogue out of fear of losing their own identity.

1. CNBB and CRB

To speak of evangelization by the CNBB without referring to the CRB (Conference of Religious of Brazil) would be to leave the picture incomplete. The more than brotherly relationship between the two Conferences needs to be stressed. They work in harmony and carry out certain projects together.

Brazil has a large number of bishops from the religious orders. These live in complete harmony with those who were diocesan priests.

2. CNBB and overseas agencies

If the Brazilian Bishops' Conference has been able to carry out beneficial work this is equally due to outside charitable agencies. The two that help above all are Adveniat Action and Suffering Church.

In conclusion, I think it can be stated that the basic problem the Conference has faced in all its evangelizing action has been the relationship between the church, the kingdom of God and the world.

The Origins of Medellín: From Catholic Action to the Base Church Communities and Social Pastoral Strategy (1950–68)

LUIZ ALBERTO GÓMEZ DE SOUZA

In this article I deal with three periods in Brazil's history: an earlier one, from 1930 to 1950; the second, as in the sub-title, from 1950 to 1968; and the following one, from 1968 to 1979. Each corresponds to a stage in socio-political and ecclesial evolution in Brazil.

The year 1930 brought the end of the old oligarchic Republic, based on coffee and with its centres of power in the states of São Paulo and Minas Gerais, through the increasing pace of industrialization and urbanization. Within the framework of an authoritarian regime, the state was modernized and labour laws were introduced. During this period, in the Catholic Church, Brazilian Catholic Action appeared, based on the Italian model, and the Dom Vital Centre in Rio de Janeiro (founded in 1922) established itself as a focus for Catholic reflection. Its central figure was Alceu Amoroso Lima, a distinguished lay intellectual, well known as a literary critic under the pen name of Tristão de Athayde, and President of Catholic Action and of the Dom Vital Centre. A recent (1928) convert to Catholicism, he had the support and encouragement of the cardinal of Rio de Janeiro, Archbishop Sebastião Leme. Unlike other South American countries, such as Chile and Venezuela, no overtly Christian political party was formed here (there was to be a Christian Democrat Party founded in 1945, but it remained somewhat marginal in the country's politics). A right-wing movement, Brazilian Integralist Action, was active between 1932 and 1938, with support from some elements in the church, but it was marginalized by both Catholic Action and the Dom Vidal Centre. There was a significant presence in cultural and indirectly in political circles through the Catholic Electoral League, of which Amoroso Lima was also president, which simply indicated which candidates were not opposed to Catholic principles and thinking.

In 1943, after the death of Cardinal Leme the previous year, Amoroso

Lima resigned from his church positions. In 1947 the priest Hélder Câmara was appointed National Assistant of Catholic Action. He was to become as dominant a figure in the church in the next period, from 1950 to 1968, as Amoroso Lima had been in the earlier one.

Catholic Action, between 1947 and 1950, following French and Canadian models, transformed itself into a grouping of specialized movements, mainly for young people, organized according to sectors of work: agricultural (JAC-JACF), educational (JEC-JECF), independent (middle sectors, JICF), manual workers (JOC-JOCF), and university (JUC).

They used the 'see-judge-act' method developed by the *Jocistes*, as well as 'life review'. The language used was of on the job training, immersion in the sector, commitment and social change. They moved from the cultural sphere and intra-church activity to active presence in society. The changes that came about in Catholic University Youth (JUC) in this period are worth noting. Organized on a national level in 1950, in 1954 the JUC embarked on a study of the social question, under the influence of Fr Lebret. Over the following years it tried to gain a better understanding of the university setting and its relationship with society. Between 1959 and 1960 it set out a 'historical ideal' for Brazil, on the lines proposed by Jacques Maritain in his *Integral Humanism*. Various groups in the country were at the time working out possible plans for the nation. But the movement later abandoned the idea of seeking a general and somewhat abstract ideal in favour of concentrating on immersing itself in the actual problems of society, under the heading of 'historical consciousness' of the moment. A Brazilian philosopher, Fr Henrique C. de Lima Vaz, collaborated in this task, and the strongest influences on the movement were Emmanuel Mounier and Pierre Teilhard de Chardin. It developed a 'community personalism', which later evolved into an option for social democracy. Former directors of the JUC and other group leaders launched a new political movement, Popular Action, which gave expression to all these tendencies in its *Documento Base* (1963).[1] The North American historian Ralph della Cava and the Chilean theologian Pablo Richard have shown that the JUC contained the seeds of a Latin American vanguard Catholicism. For Gustavo Gutiérrez, this is where the first seeds of what was later to become liberation theolgy germinated.[2]

In 1952 Dom Hélder Câmara, by then auxiliary bishop of Rio de Janeiro, created and became first General Secretary of the National Conference of Brazilian Bishops (CNBB), a pioneering organ in the church, which formulated church structures on the national level. Until then, throughout the world, these had followed the mediaeval format of local diocese-Rome link and were at the time trying adapt themselves to the modern dimensions of the nation-state. In forming the CNBB, Dom Hélder made use of what he had learned from Catholic Action, which he used as a working model for its operations. To do so, he leant on Catholic Action directors, mainly women, who were thus at the very origin of the Bishops' Conference. This lay and female influence has not always been taken into account.[3]

Dom Hélder, with the collaboration of the bishops of the north east, organized meetings in the region to study its most pressing problems (1951, 1952). These meetings gave rise to the suggestions that led President Kubitschek to create the Superintendency for Development of the North East (SUDENE), headed by the then young economist Celso Furtado. The gatherings of bishops from the north dealt with the problems of Amazonia (1952, 1957). In 1960, on the basis of diocesan experiences in educational radio, Dom José Távora, archbishop of Aracaju and formerly, like Dom Hélder, auxiliary bishop of Rio and the new President, Jânio Quadros, worked out an agreement between the CNBB and the Ministry of Education, which led to the creation of the Base Education Movement (MEB). This was to become one of the most important and creatives centres for mass education, with literacy campaigns carried out over the radio. It was in the MEB that there developed a practice of and reflection on education and popular culture, complementary to similar initiatives, such as that undertaken by Paulo Freire, first in Pernambuco and then throughout the country, or by the Popular Culture Movement (MCP) in Recife, or the Popular Culture Centre (CPC) of the National Student Union, and many other bodies. Through the MEB, the church was to have a presence in this pioneering Brazilian enterprise, which after the coup was to spread throughout Latin America and around the world.

All this change took place in the context of a broader social, economic, and cultural process in the nation. Between 1950 and 1964, from the second Vargas government (1950–4) to the military coup, two key concepts dominated: nationalism and development. The first sought to affirm Brazil as a nation, define its identity, and redesign the fragile structures of a peripheral country. At the same time, the process of industrialization placed the notion of development at the centre of the debate, carried on then through regional bodies such as the Economic Commission for Latin America (CEPAL). The concerns were then studied by the Higher Institute for Brazilian Studies (ISEB), which was linked to the presidency of the Republic. It was the era of the 'Target Plan' of Juscelino Kubitschek's government (1955–9) and the building of Brasilia. There was an overall climate of optimism and hope.

Then, between 1961 and 1963, came proposals for social reforms that could not be delayed. A message from the Central Commission of the CNBB, dated 30 April 1963, less than a year before the military coup, declared: 'Our society is, still, vitiated by the heavy burden of a capitalist tradition . . . a state of affairs in which economic power, money, still exercises the ultimate authority over economic, political, and social decisions.' It went on to demand a 'transition to another social structure in which persons recover their full human dimension'. It followed this by suggesting reforms in the following areas: land, business, administration, justice, elections, education. This text, read in today's context of free-market, economicist, and conservative thinking, still has a tremendous relevance.[4]

In 1962 the CNBB, inspired by the beginnings of the Second Vatican Council, launched the idea of an 'emergency plan' for the church. It started from the challenges posed by the situation '. . . of the overwhelming dictatorship of the economic sphere and of the egoism of present structures, which neutralize our efforts at christianization'. It began a trial of 'overall pastoral care', which was strengthened and defined in the following years, linking pastoral activities to the situation in the country.[5] Between 1962 and 1964, lay Christians took part in a large number of programmes of popular education, rural trade unions, and university reform. It is true that this aroused reactions and fears in conservative sectors of the church, which denounced it in the press. The same had happened in 1960, when Dom Hélder Câmara, faced with criticism of the activities of the JUC, sent a note to the bishops saying that this movement, 'far from being exorbitant . . . has seen its time come and deserves support and encouragement from your excellencies the bishops'.

Positions became polarized. Groups in the church organized 'Marches with God, for the Family and for Freedom', denouncing a left-wing threat, while other groups took part in reform movements. With the coup of 1 April 1964, the former supported the military, and some took places in the government of General Castello Branco; the latter were obliged to suspend their activities, some being interrogated by police and imprisoned or forced into exile.[6]

Following the coup, Dom Hélder Câmara was transferred to the diocese of Olinda and Recife and had to resign as general secretary of the CNBB. There were drastic changes affecting the whole conduct of the nation and of the church. In his column in the press, Alceu Amoroso Lima, still a respected lay intellectual, denounced the repression and what he called 'cultural terrorism'.[7] The episcopate was divided 'by the umbilical cord', as one analyst said.[8] The JUC was the first to feel the difficulties of the new situation. Under pressures from within the CNBB, between 1966 and 1967, its national co-ordinatination was eliminated, and the movement virtually disappeared.

Even in July 1966, however, despite censorship and purges, the review *Paz e Terra* appeared, inspired by John XXIII's encyclical *Pacem in Terris*, and produced by evangelical Christians, Catholics, and Marxists. The subtitle proclaimed: 'Ecumenism and humanism; encounter and dialogue'. The climate in the church a year after the end of Vatican II allowed this exercise to be carried out. The first number contained articles by Amoroso Lima, Fr Henrique de Lima Vaz, Luiz Eduardo Wanderley, and the present writer.[9]

In 1965 Hélder Câmara, returning from the final session of the council, in dialogue with Ivan Illich, director of the Intercultural Documentation Center of Cuernavaca (CIDOC), suggested that it was now time to begin to prepare for a new council, a possible Vatican III.[10] And, in correspondence with Dom Manuel Larraín, the Chilean bishop of Talca and president of the Latin America Council of Bishops (CELAM), he launched the idea of a regional meeting to apply the council resolutions. This is how the 1968 Medellín meeting came into being, but, instead of a mere application of the council, it proved to be a true 'regional council or synod', like those that were held in the East in the early centuries of the church. It took a step forward, in its critique of an unequal society, in its denunciation of 'social sin', in its proclamation of the poor as the preferential option, and in its opening out of a broad and evangelical perspective of liberation.

Elsewhere, 1968 was an especially significant year on many levels. Throughout the world, counter-cultural and youth rebellion movements broke out, especially on university campuses. Not only in Paris, Berkeley, Columbia, or Prague, but also in the Catholic University of Santiago de Chile, after it had been taken over by the students, there began a creative experiment in reform, led by the Brazilian philosopher Ernani Maria Fiori, a leading *gaucho* layman, exiled from his country. In Brazil, however, on 13 December of that year, the regime was stiffened, with a coup within the coup, by the passing of Institutional Act no. 5. For many years, this closed off spaces of relative freedom that had survived precariously from 1964. There followed a period of repression, uprisings, torture, and 'disappearing' of political leaders. The church denounced the military's doctrine of national security and, through Bishop Cândido Padim and his Justice and Peace Commissions, acted as a valiant defender of human rights. This is when it became 'the voice of the voiceless'. Those difficult years saw the birth and development of the CEBs, and the publication of the social pastorals on land (1975), indigenous peoples (1975), industrial workers, young people, and so on. This was the period when, standing out against an extremely repressive and stifling civil panorama in the region (Pinochet's coup in Chile in 1973, coups in Argentina and Uruguay), the church in Latin America, between the Medellín conference in 1968 and Puebla in 1979, lived through what might be called a 'glorious decade' in its practice, creativity, and prophetic presence.[11]

This was the beginning of a new period, for which the ground had undoubtedly been prepared, as we have seen, by specialized Catholic Action, by the CNBB, by the prophetic presence of Hélder Câmara, and by the involvement of so many Christians in social and ecclesial activities. The CEBs and the social pastorals of the following years were in turn part of the beginning of renewal of the trade union movement, the rise of the Worker's Party in 1980, and of so many new social movements, including the Landless Workers Movement (MST; late 1980s), womens's, ethnic, and ecological movements. They all formed a dense network of Christian practices that, in the Brazil of the period, bore witness to the vital and evangelical relationship between faith and everyday life.

Notes

1. L. G. Souza Lima, *Evolução política dos católicos e da Igreja no Brasil*, Petrópolis 1979; G. Semeraro, *A primavera dos anos sessenta. A geração de Betinho*, São Paulo 1994. After the coup Popular Action clandestinely turned itself into a Marxist movement, turning its back on its origins.

2. L. A. Gómez de Souza, *A JUC: os estudantes católicos e a política*, Petrópolis 1985; R. Della Cava, 'Catholicism and society in twentieth century Brazil' in *Latin American Research Review*, 2, 11; P. Richard, *Death of Christendom and Birth of the Church*, Maryknoll, NY 1987; R. Diaz-Salazar, *La izquierda y el cristianismo*, Madrid 1998.

3. As we commemorate fifty years of the CNBB in 2002, we should recall the close links in Rio between the national lay secretariat of Catholic Action, in rua México, and the secretariat of the CNBB, in the São Joaquim na Glória palace. On the other hand, the Synod of Bishops in 2001 showed how, half a century later, the church still finds it difficult to integrate and strengthen the collegial structures of national conferences and apply to itself the principle of subsidiarity it puts forward for civil society. This church, in the hands of the clergy and centralized in the Roman Curia for the whole of the last millennium, shows internal resistance and inertia militating against the institutional *aggiornamento* it needs for it to integrate the laity and new national dimensions.

4. L. E. Wanderley, *Educar para transformar*, Petrópolis 1984; E. de Kadt, *Catholic Radicals in Brazil*, London 1970.

5. S. Mainwaring, *The Catholic Church and Politics in Brazil*, Stanford 1986; T. Bruneau, *Catolicismo brasileiro em época de transição*, São Paulo 1974.

6. R. C. de Barros, *Brasil. Uma Igreja em renovação*, Petrópolis 1967.

7. M. Moreira Alves, *O Cristo do povo*, Rio de Janeiro 1968.

8. Article with this title, May 1964. See A. Amoroso Lima, *Revolução, reação ou reforma?* Crônicas de 1958 a 1964, Petrópolis ²1999.

9. C. Antoine, *L'Église et le pouvoir au Brésil*, Paris 1971.

10. In this post-conciliar climate I went to work at Cuernavaca, in 1965, dreaming of a possible Vatican III. I expressed this in conversation with Amoroso Lima (see my article 'Amoroso Lima, na permanente preparação da Idade Nova. Reflexões a partir de uma carta sua' in *Revista Eclesiástica Brasileira* 43 (Dec. 1983).

11. L. A. Gómez de Souza 'A caminhada de Medellín a Puebla' in *Perspectiva Teológica* 84 (May-Aug. 1999).

Stories of Faith and Life in the Base Communities

FAUSTINO TEIXEIRA

Introduction

The Base Church Communities (CEBs) constitute one of the richest and most meaningful experiences the Brazilian church has to offer the universal church. This new way of 'being church' that is developing in Brazil expresses the great dynamism of our church life,[1] revealing and indicating particular facets of a church committed to affirming life and the cause of the poor. At the beginning of the 1980s Karl Rahner, lamenting the winter situation of the church, could still point to the alternative presence of the Christianity pulsating in Latin America, marked by determination and witness, an experience 'rich in great hopes'.[2] In effect, the experience of the base communities has encouraged the genesis of a new face of the church, characterized by its features of communion, commitment, and participation and marked by the dynamic of following Jesus Christ. Throughout these nearly forty years of their course, the CEBs in Brazil have emphasized the essential imperative of opting for the poor and for their right to citizenship in society and in the church. This is a summons issued to the whole people of God, in the sense of moving to adopt the viewpoint of the church of the poor: 'All are called to intense participation in brotherly communion and the integration of faith in history on the basis of the actual situation and real life'.[3] During the course of their history, the CEBs have built up experience and faced fresh challenges as well as misunderstanding and opposition. Perhaps the greatest richness of this church experience is to be found in its potential for dialogue and its capacity for permanent rebirth, which indicate its potential for openness to the new horizons that continually open up throughout history.

I. A story of faith and life

The base communities in Brazil were born in the context of the ferment in society that marked the beginning of the 1960s. At this time, the national scene – social, cultural, and ecclesial – was distinguished by the active presence of movements such as Catholic Action (especially the JUC, JEC, and JOC) and the Basic Education Movement (MEB). Such movements planted the first seeds of a critical understanding of the gospel and of the effect of faith on history. They created the conditions for redefining what was meant by Christians adopting a critical stance within both the church and Brazilian society, posing key questions that both prefigured and anticipated the themes that were later to emerge in liberation theology and the base church communities. The military coup of 1964 and its consequences blocked this process, but it could not hinder the dynamic of pastoral initiatives being pursued in the shanty-towns around the major cities and in rural areas. The communities were born out of this difficult political situation, like a little 'defenceless flower', simple and basic in form, enabling the poor and excluded to express themselves on the basis of reflection on the Bible. The decisive motivation came from the wider church circumstances: this was the springtime of the immediate post-Vatican II years, immediately backed up by the new challenges posed by the Medellín Conference in 1968.

In the 1970s the CEB experiment spread throughout the whole of Brazil, experiencing a period of great vitality. Through the power of witness and example, many experiences were spread far and wide, guaranteed by their truth to the radical gospel message. People were seeking a renewed church, one capable of taking up the problems, difficulties, and joys of the impoverished masses: an adult community, committed to Christ but equally to the people and their liberation; a community inspired by the Spirit and distinguished by a life of communion and of brotherly help. This period saw the rise of the Inter-Church Meetings of CEBs, which were basic to the maturing and spread of the experiment.

During the 1980s the communities in Brazil faced a series of new challenges, related to the changes in the overall situation of the country as reflected in both politics and the church. One of the central themes in this period concerned the *question of the ecclesial nature of the CEBs*. New winds from the international ecclesiastical circumstances were no longer set fair for the experiments being made. This was the start of a time of 'restoration' in the Catholic Church, with painful repercussions for the whole liberationist pastoral approach in Latin America and for the CEBs in particular. The logic of the centralizing approach taken by Rome from this time on was to leave its marks on the Brazilian church. Its most innovative experiments were the focus of attention, criticism, and misunderstanding. In many cases, the CEBs were chosen as the prime target for attack, but the overall aim was at the process of evangelization then being pursued in Brazil and its resounding critique of unjust societies. The opposition and attacks were designed to obstruct or eclipse the church in Brazil, which was then emerging as a creative and prophetic church in the eyes of other countries. The obstructions and misunderstandings increased in proportion to the centralization and imposition of uniformity in the ruling church model.[4]

Since the end of the 1980s new horizons and challenges have been opening up, broadening the communities' sphere of interests, such as the areas of culture, ethnicity, gender, individuality, ecology, spirituality, ecumenism, and so on. These are themes that 'broaden their vision, sometimes with difficulty, but always within the framework of their not-to-be-renounced options within the social conflict'.[5] The broadening of horizons does not mean the communities are losing their vitality: they are still 'alive and on track'. The harsh, conflictive situation produced by the advance of free-market ideology, not to mention back-tracking in the church, may produce a certain 'deceleration' here and there, but this does not signify any loss of the vitality of the experience. The various regional assemblies of the CEBs and the accounts given by their 'animators' all over Brazil testify to the presence of a real dynamism, which can be understood only by those who follow the experience closely and believe in the power of its spirituality.

II. A conversion experience in the way of being church

The new way of being church in the communities involves a significant change in the field of religious experience for those who are part of them. It would be quite appropriate to call it a conversion, as it represents a marked change in both one's personal and collective experience of religion itself.[6] The characteristics of converts in the CEBs are different from those who follow the two other recognized courses of conversion: those who change religions, and those who discover a religion without ever having belonged to one before. In the case of the CEBs, individuals can be seen to re-affiliate to the same tradition, to rediscover a new religious identity even though they adhered formally to it before. Joining a base community involves its members in entry into a 'strong regime of intense religiosity', which produces an ethical and spiritual re-assessment of their whole life.[7]

Members of communities come to share in a new identity, reorganizing their 'converse apparatus' on new lines. A substantial portion of the new internalization of religion promoted by the CEBs consists of a new relationship with the sacred, which now implies the centrality of conscientization, a new ethical and political commitment, and stress on sharing in the people's struggles. The feeling of belonging to the community brings with it a new view of the world, a new symbolic horizon, and other collective practices. Becoming part of its journey means identifying oneself with a new way of being Catholic that presupposes consistent ethical and social commitment to the project of affirming life.

The process of change implied by this new church outlook produces significant changes, which can be summed up as a *dynamic of participating*. The CEBs have initiated new ways for lay people to participate in the life of faith, in services, and in the organization of the community. They come to see themselves as 'ecclesial subjects', breaking the previous 'clerical monopoly' of power, and they make themselves responsible for carrying out the various services called for by new historical needs. It is worth emphasizing the substantial role played by women, whose part in the communities is inspiring and fundamental, involving all fields of their experience. Research carried out in the 1980s and 1990s in Brazilian dioceses, including the experiences of the CEBs, nevertheless shows that there are well-defined limits to this participation, which point to the fragile situation occupied by the communities within the institutional church. There is evidence of a lack of procedures by which the influence of decisions taken by lay people can extend beyond merely local limits.

This participation is not restricted to church life but extends into *endeavour in society*. The communities stress the essential nature of the ties binding following Jesus to the struggle for transforming society. Humanization is a decisive criterion in the way the communities operate and in their manner of assessing the value of religious experience. The communities have always distinguished the centrality of witness for the kingdom of God, which must necessarily involve affirming the life of the little ones and those excluded from society. Openness to the social question is a congenital feature of the CEBs. This approach and requirement stem from the motivating relationship between and life found in the popular biblical hermeneutics practised in the communities. As a result of this commitment, not a few animators and pastoral agents working in the CEBs have undergone the experience of martyrdom. This confirmed 'martyrial practice' within the communities has from the time of their origins proved an expression of the evangelically radical nature of their experience. And these martyrs are alive in the communities: in their celebrations, in their language, in reliquaries and so many other symbols that adorn members' houses, clothes, and places of worship. As Bishop Pedro Casaldáliga has pointed out, 'A church that forgot its martyrs would not deserve to survive.'[8]

III. The centrality of the Bible

One element given prominence in all relevant studies of the CEBs is the place allotted to the Bible in the communities' experience. It forms their 'founding nucleus', the element that identifies their way of being church. It has become the basis from which the communities draw their sustenance and their vitality, the nucleus from which the motivational universe of the impoverished is formed. It was from Bible study that the first base communities emerged, in the form of 'Bible circles' or 'Gospel groups' in the 1960s, and this basis reference has continued to sustain them on their communal journey.

The CEBs introduced a new biblical hermeneutics, one that delivers a liberating reading of the word of God. This is an interpretation dynamized by the option in favour of the poor, which produces a close bond between the word and the life of the people. The biblical reading is thereby enriched by the con-text of the community and by the pre-text of the general situation. The result is always novel and motivational. The real problems that affect the lives of the people have fresh light shed on them by the world, which goes to work in the community, showing their meaning and giving guidance on the way to tackle them. The new approach enables the poor to see the Bible as a familiar book reflecting their own situation as if in a mirror, and they take fresh stock of this word, which comes to signify the source of inspiration and life for them. In recent years, the communities have to enrich their popular reading with the prayer dimension of the word: the Bible has become a source for prayer and for deepening their spirituality. Alongside their familiarity with the Bible, they are developing a deeper appreciation of its aspect of gift and of its otherness.

On the basis of their biblical reflections, the communities are opening the way for an all-embracing spirituality, identified as the spirituality of following Jesus. This embodies a threefold spiritual experience inspired by the dynamic relationship between three elements: *involvement* in and *commitment* to the world of the impoverished and *closeness* to the Lord of history. This is an experience that involves at once awareness of the presence of

Christ in one's poor brothers and sisters and openness to the free gift of God's mystery, which leads to a more decisive and less encumbered presence on the stage of history.

IV. An identity being built

Certain sectors of the media and the intelligentsia see the CEBs as now going through a stage of exhaustion and crisis. In the Brazilian case, the reasons usually advanced for this 'reflux' involve the growth of evangelical Pentecostal churches and infiltration by Catholic Charismatic Renewal. There is in fact no denying that growth on the evangelical Pentecostal wing has produced a shift in the Brazilian religious scene, resulting in a weakening of the 'character of hegemonic definer of truth and of institutional identity' previously held by the Catholic Church.[9]

As part of this religious scene, the CEBs also come up against this question of Pentecostal growth; they do not necessarily see it as a threat but rather as a challenge to broaden their ecumenical and inter-religious appeal. This basic approach has surfaced in lively debate at recent Inter-Church community meetings. At the ninth of these, held in the city of São Luis do Maranhão in 1997, one of the subject groups dealt with just this question of dialogue with Pentecostals and Catholic Charismatics. What emerged was the challenge of finding a way to live together on a daily basis and to work out a common strategy for actions and specific struggles on behalf of the poor.

The CEBs have never claimed a massive outreach but have always sought to favour working together as a community, which is a qualitative aim and guarantees bonds of fellowship among their members. The quantitative reach of their pastoral presence has never exceeded about 9% of the local population of the dioceses in which they are present, and there are varying levels of involvement in a base community. Their great power-house is the nucleus of 'animators' – male and female. Then there are those who take part in one or more of the community's activities, then those who confine their participation to eucharistic celebrations. The combination of animators and participants is what characterizes the communities and between them accounts for no more than 9% of the local population. One of the challenges faced by the communities in the field of mass pastoral endeavour is how to integrate those distanced from the dynamic nucleus into the communities in a more definite fashion.[10]

Taking part in the Inter-Church Meetings of the CEBs allows one to appreciate the process of building the communities' ecclesial identity. Even if they are not really typical of the daily experience of life in the communities, since they express their celebratory and festive aspect, such gatherings do show their ecclesial dynamic and present and developing tendencies. These meetings began in 1975, aimed at producing a greater coherence among all the communities spread throughout Brazil. The tenth took place in the city of Ilhéus in Lower Amazonia, with some 3,600 people attending. What it discovered was not a crisis among the CEBs but a re-assessment of their place in society and in the church in the light of the new challenges evident at the dawn of the new millennium. As one of those who reported on the meeting wrote: 'The CEBs are lively because they are experimental, agile, and varied.'[11] They have not become fossilized or set in stone but are always 'switched on' and open to new horizons. Beyond the limitations of their understanding of the present situation, they are open to understanding what might become possible, pointing out untried repertoires that are nonetheless vital to the life of the church at the present time.

The latest meeting in Ilhéus took the temperature of the present climate of the CEBs, emphasizing the major questions raised by their experience to date.[12] The *ecumenical and inter-religious* question is being set on firmer foundations, indicating a growing acceptance of otherness. The increasingly obvious presence of Afro-Brazilian religions and of the indigenous question has encouraged the communities to make a different assessment of inculturation. This is now being understood as not mere adaptation but as creative interpretation. The dynamics of encounter with such traditions is leading to a re-interpretation of the content of Christianity itself, favouring the emergence of a new face of the church. A fresh macro-ecumenical sensitivity is encouraging the communities to open their arms wider, so as to embrace diversity more intensely, recognizing it as an expression of the vast riches of the God who is ever greater. And communion in diversity leads to a search for a common and more decided commitment to defending threatened life.

The meeting at Ilhés placed equal emphasis on the importance of deepening the *ministerial function* in the communities. The dream of an all-ministerial church has always been part of the CEBs, but it has been progressively more emphasized in recent years. In contradistinction to the centralizing tendency now seen in the Catholic Church, the communities are stubbornly pointing in a different direction, believing in the dream of a fully participative and wholly ministerial church. Their defence of this stance was strengthened at Ilhéus by the contributions made by women, who stressed the need for a greater sharing and distribution of power in the church and particularly their presence on the different levels of service and decision-making. Related to this ministerial question, the subject of the communities' *right to the eucharist* was also raised. This is one of the most delicate questions, but one that is increasingly coming to the fore with the vitality shown by the Brazilian communities. The CEBs define themselves as celebratory communities, but they still find themselves largely cut off from the possibility of celebrating the eucharist. Figures show that 70% of Sunday celebrations in the communities are held without a priest. This situation raises a serious question for theology and church discipline, as another commentator on the CEBs has noted: 'There is the problem of examining the question of what the real eucharistic presence means in celebrations without an ordained minister.'[13] The ministerial experience reflected in the CEBs points to the urgency of a deeper reflection on lay leadership and the scope and activities of new, non-ordained ministers.

The base communities are still alive and stubbornly clinging to their dream of a church more attuned to following Jesus and bringing in the kingdom of God, of a church that makes the option for history and for those excluded by that history, of a church that demonstrates solidarity and welcome, of a witness church. The ecclesiastical winds are not blowing particularly favourably at the moment, but the communities are used to surviving more difficult situations, and history has taught them the stratagems needed to keep the flame of their hope within their reach.

Notes

1. CNBB, *As comunidades eclesiais de base na Igreja do Brasil*, 4th ed. São Paulo 1986, n.1.
2. K. Rahner, *Confessare la fede nel tempo dell'attesa*, Rome 1994, p.230.
3. CNBB, *As comunidades eclesiais*, n.51.
4. C. Quieróz, *Igreja no Brasil – Anos 80. Evolução da CNBB: documentos e posições, Rio de Janeiro* (mimeo, Aug. 1985), p.6.
5. L. A. Gómez de Souza, 'As CEBs vão bem, obrigado' in *REB* 60 (2000), p.107.
6. F. Teixeira, 'A espiritualidade nas CEBs', in C. Boff et al., *As comunidades de base em questão*, São Paulo 1997, pp.208–9.
7. D. Hervieu-Léger, *Le pèlerin et le converti: la religion en mouvement*, Paris 1999, pp.124–5.
8. P. Casaldáliga & J. M. Vigil, *Espiritualidade da libertação*, Petrópolis 1993, p.182; Eng. trans. *The Spirituality of Liberation*, Tunbridge Wells and Maryknoll, NY 1994.
9. P. Sanchis, 'O repto pentecostal à "cultura católica brasileira"', in A. Antoniazzi et al., *Nem anjos nem demônios: interpretações sociológicas do pentecostalismo*, Petrópolis 1994, p.36.

10. P. A. Ribeiro de Oliveira, 'CEB: unidade estruturante de Igreja', in C. Boff et al., *As comunidades* (n.6), pp.145–6.
11. L. A. Gómez de Souza, 'As CEBs vão bem, obrigado' (n.5), p.107.
12. F. Teixeira, 'O resgate e a afirmação de um sonho: o X Encontro Intereclesial de CEBs' in *Perspectiva Teológica* 88 (2000), pp.393–413.
13. J. B. Libânio, 'O X Encontro Intereclesial de CEBs: leitura teológica' in REB 60 (2000), p.552.

The Struggle for Modern and Ancestral Rights: Thirty Years of the Indianist Missionary Council (CIMI)

PAULO SUESS

I. Historical panorama of the rise of CIMI

In April 1972 the Brazilian National Bishops Conference (CNBB) called together a group of missionary bishops to advise it on questions of 'The Status of the Indian', which was under discussion in the Chamber of Deputies.[1] The condemnations uttered by anthropologists gathered in January 1971 at the 'Symposium on inter-ethnic friction in South America' held in Barbados also had repercussions within the CNBB.[2] These condemnations held that ' the ethnocentric content of the evangelizing activity' of the religious missions was based on 'their essentially discriminatory nature' and on their economic power, which meant that the missions were becoming 'recolonization and domination' businesses. In May 1970 thirty-two bishops from Amazonia declared the condemnations of genocide of the Indians in Brazil 'exaggerated' and showed their support for the Indianist policies of the military government led by General Médici (1969–74). The building of the Trans-Amazonian highway was beginning to cast its first shadows over twenty-nine indigenous peoples.

The group of advisers convened by the CNBB was later formed into a national body planning and co-ordinating missionary outreach to the indigenous peoples, in the shape of an Indianist Missionary Council (CIMI). This came into being seven years after Vatican II and four years after Medellín.[3] By statute, all those who work directly or indirectly in the church's pastoral mission to the indigenous peoples are under the auspices of CIMI.

CIMI came into being too late to have a decisive influence on the 'Indian Statute'. The article in the Statute that delegated the right to provide aid services for the Indians to religious and scientific bodies fell victim to a veto by President Médici on 19 December 1973. He based this on the 1969

Constitution of the military regime, which enabled him to veto any proposal
by the legislature. In his message no. 530/73, justifying the use of the veto,
the president declared that the 'cardinal objectives of the Statute' consisted
precisely in the 'rapid and salutary integration of the Indian into civilization'.

The exclusive reservation to the state of the right to provide aid services
for the indigenous peoples was the root cause of later conflicts between the
state with its National Foundation for the Indian (Funai) on the one hand,
and the church and civil society on the other. Funai was the successor agency
to the 'Service of Protection to the Indian' (SPI), founded in 1910 and closed
down on account of corruption in 1967. The 'Figueiredo Report'[4] blamed
the SPI for the massacres of entire tribes by dynamiting, machine-gunning,
and poisoning. Funai, which took over the positivist philosophy of the military and inherited many officers from the defunct SPI, was in legal terms the
'tutelary body' of the indigenous peoples. In the Indianist legislation of the
time, the Indians were 'legally' under tutelage and their tutelage would end
with their integration into the dominant culture of Brazil.

At the time CIMI was founded, however, thirty years ago, neither
Brazilian society nor the local churches, on the whole, believed that the
indigenous peoples could have a future of their own. The indigenous question, as such, was generally regarded as a 'lost cause'. It seemed logical that
the obvious course for the 180,000 Indians living at the time would be to
become integrated into the cultural and juridical patterns of the nation's
dominant society and assimilated into its ethnicity and religion. The
integrationist approach removed the need to demarcate Indian lands and
provide specific protection for them.

Following the pastoral guidelines set out at Medellín and the contributions made by a post-colonial anthropology, and reacting against the anti-
popular authoritarianism of the military regime, a significant section of the
missionary community made its 'option for the indigenous people'. From
1974 on, CIMI facilitated meetings among indigenous leaders, not only
in Brazil but throughout Amerindia, from which sprang autonomous
organizations with new political and theological views. Obviously, this
option brought conflict, not only with the state but also within some local
churches. The question of where the indigenous peoples were going was
what most divided opinion. The killing of indigenous leaders common in the
past was from then on supplemented with the killing of missionaries, men
and women. The Salesian Rudolf Lunkenbein, one of the first missionaries
to belong to the recently founded CIMI, was also the first to be murdered

(on 15 July 1976), in the struggle over the demarcation of the territory of 'his' Bororo people. Others were to follow.[5]

A just solution to the question of Indian lands would require profound changes to the ruling economic and social-political model, based as it is on profit, authoritarianism, and the arbitrary will of the strongest, and working through its mechanisms of integration into classist society. In this debate, CIMI's philosophy advocates a future of their own for the indigenous peoples, which would require a specific, integral and widely co-ordinated pastoral strategy. It has shown that it is possible to respond in both pastoral and political terms to the historical challenges built up over centuries.

II. The indigenous cause and the land question

Comparing the present indigenous population of over 500,000 with the 180,000 in 1972 shows that the 225 indigenous peoples who inhabit Brazilian land are among the fastest growing segments of the population. Of these 500,000, who between them speak 180 different languages, around 385,000 live on their own lands, while over 190,000 have migrated to urban conglomerations, where an uncertain future awaits them.[6] In the last thirty years several indigenous tribes, considered extinct by official surveys, have reappeared. It was not CIMI that 'invented' these peoples, as some un-informed sources have alleged, but it has been CIMI's work that has contributed, among other factors, to the social climate in which the 're-appearance' of more than fifty 'resuscitated peoples' can be accepted.[7]

At the present time, over thirty different denominations and/or churches, with markedly differing outlooks, have a presence alongside the indigenous peoples. Sometimes, as a strategy for gaining social acceptance, the Indians allow Christianity to overlay the ancient religions, which continue to distinguish their identity in a collective clandestinity. In this respect, Curt Nimuendaju tells a significant story of what happened when his adoptive father from the Guaraní people was presented to the governor of the state of São Paulo in 1902:

> Then the [Catholic] priest comes to visit me in the village; I receive him as best I can, ordering a chicken to be killed for him and, at night, a bed to be made ready for him. The next morning he tells what he knows, this and that; when he finishes, I say 'Yes, Sir'; he is satisfied . . . and says: 'This captain, yes, this is a good captain!' – Then when the [Protestant] minister comes, I also have a chicken killed for him . . .; he also tells me his

story and I listen and reply: 'Yes, Sir, Mr Minister.' And then he is satis-
fied and says: 'This one, yes, this is a true captain!' And that is how I treat
them all.[8]

In order to defend their lands and their cultures, many indigenous
peoples today have two religions: Christianity to relate 'politically' to
surrounding society, and their own religion for celebrating life's events.

Autonomous indigenous societies, with their subsistence way of life, are
distinguished from Brazilian society principally by the land question: by the
origin of its appropriation (primary possession, not purchase); by the practical use they make of it (subsistence cultivation); by their structure (collective
property); and by their religious view of it (sacred land). This land is not just
a 'means of production'. It is the setting for the collective memory of the
people, of their history, of their leisure and work; it is where they celebrate
their rites of life and death. For the indigenous peoples, all the separate
questions of their liberation and resistance come together in the question of
land.

The Brazilian Constitution promulgated on 5 October 1988 promised the
indigenous peoples, within five years, the demarcation of their lands and
some other basic rights. But many of the Constitution's legal provisions, the
product of broad consensus between the indigenous peoples and progressive
sectors of society, still remain paper promises. Decree 1775, from 1996,
which regulates the procedure for demarcating indigenous lands, seriously
damaged this process by allowing legal challenges to be mounted by illegal
invaders of indigenous lands. This demarcation process is now the subject of
a complex juridical inquiry.

Brazilian legislation distinguishes three categories of indigenous lands.
The first is *lands traditionally occupied* by the indigenous peoples. According
to the Federal Constitution of 1988 (article 231, para. 1) these lands belong
to the state. The Indians' rights of possession and use over these lands and
the natural riches of their soil, rivers, and lakes are original: that is, they
derive from the traditional indigenous occupation itself, which antedates the
formation of the Brazilian state. The second category is that of *reserved lands*,
dealt with by the 'Indian Statute' of 1973 (articles 26 to 31), still in force.
These reserved lands are Reservations, Farming Colonies, and Federal
Indigenous Territories. They are created by the state, generally for indigenous peoples or communities that have irretrievably lost their traditionally
occupied lands, as when they have been submerged under the reservoirs of
hydro-electric schemes, for example. The third category is that of *owned*

lands ('Indian Statute', articles 32 and 33): that is, those lands that belong to specific indigenous communities that have acquired them through civil law processes (purchase, donation, usucaption).

Making indigenous lands legally secure means subjecting their inhabitants to a lengthy process of bureaucratic procedures, from initial reports by a Technical Group to publication in the Union Official Bulletin. The only lands that are legally secure – or demarcated – are those approved through publication of the Homologation Decree signed by the president and published in the Union Official Bulletin. These lands have to be marked on official maps and registered with the Department of the Patrimony of the Union.

According to figures from CIMI, only 236 out of of 756 indigenous territories are effectively guaranteed, in the sense that the whole demarcation process is complete, while no measures have been taken over 178. Bearing in mind that, for the indigenous peoples, all separate questions of their liberation and resistance converge in the question of land, the struggle for indigenous territories is the vital element in a strategy of integral evangelization.

III. An alternative vision and reciprocal learning

The struggle to preserve the diversity of species, including the human species, is also a struggle for the liberation of Planet Earth. The indigenous cause brings a new logic to social and ecological relationships. The indigenous peoples are struggling for different scientific, technological, and political priorities. After the long period of colonization, and after the military dictatorships in Latin America, practically all nation-states have become constitutional. The 'indigenous cause' has to be considered within the framework of all these states, despite the fragile nature of their institutions, caused partly by their lack of democratic tradition but increasingly by the macro-structure shaped by free-market global capitalism with its paucity of meaning.

Globalization of relationships requires, besides the perfectioning of each sector of the globe, codes of common understanding and action to combat the trans-cultural scourges of hunger, violence, unemployment, and social exclusion. Defence of the indigenous peoples cannot be mounted on the basis of a pre-, post-, or extra-modern political project. The indigenous peoples' view of life opens up new horizons within and beyond the achievements of modernity. The projects of the indigenous peoples themselves throw fresh lights on achievements such as self-reliance and autonomy, citizenship and democratic participation in the nation's decision-making, sharing with one's equals in the process of becoming a subject while remaining distinct, as well as on prospects that also include future generations. The indigenous peoples accept the achievements of modernity (citizenship, participation, self-determination), but at the same time they critique the hegemonic appropriation of the benefits of this modernity by communications empires, by conquerors, and by élites. This critique adds power and voices to those of the 'Third Subject', the powerless majorities within every society.

In their cultural utopias, the indigenous peoples make people think of the essence of life as a gift they contemplate on a river bank or on seeing others. This was certainly why the Catholic Church in Brazil decided on 'Brotherhood and Indigenous Peoples' as the theme for its 2002 Brotherhood Campaign, in an endeavour to awaken the Christian communities and civil society to a sense of their responsibility for the indigenous peoples' struggle for their lands, for their identity, and for the chance of a life worthy of the name. The political goals of this project are citizenship, sharing, and freedom as equals in their difference: citizenship against domination and exclusion; sharing against exploitation; equality in difference against the monotony of poverty and the mono-culture of the rule of the market.

Today the indigenous cultures combine 'neolithic' and 'modern' aspects, mythological explanations and historical visions of their resistance and political struggle. Myth and history, magic and science can shape complementary visions of the world.[9] The modern world too cannot explain reality without recourse to myths. Thanks to Freud, the Oedipus myth has become an explanation for the human condition in the modern age. The 'big bang' with which scientists today explain the origin of the cosmos is as mythic as the birth of the first human couple from inside a stone, as the *Mynky* people's myth tells. The different order of things within the indigenous world compared to the 'modern world' can also serve as a complementary and alternative order for the human race. Indigenous peoples make us think about the essentials of life, hidden 'this side of thought and on the far side of society: in contemplating a mineral more beautiful than anything we can make; in a scent wiser than all our books, breathed in the heart of a lily; or in the wink of an eye, full of patience, calm, and mutual forgiveness that an unconscious understanding sometimes allows one to exchange with a cat'.[10]

Notes

1. See 'Gênese do Estatuto do Índio' in P. Suess, *Cálice e cuia*, Petrópolis 1985, pp.42–9.
2. The text of the manifesto of the 'Symposium on inter-ethnic friction in South America' is in P. Suess (ed.), *Em defesa dos povos indígenas*, São Paulo 1980, pp.19–26.
3. See P. Suess, *A causa indígena na caminhada e proposta do Cimi: 1972–1989*, Petrópolis 1989.
4. The 'Figueiredo Report', containing 5,115 pages of denunciations, was published in March 1968, by the Minister of the Interior, General Albuquerque Lima.
5. P. Suess, 'Rodolfo Lunkenbein (1939–1976). Asesinado por oponerse al exterminio de los indios,' in E. Stehle (ed.), *Testigos de la fe en América Latina desde el descubrimiento hasta nuestros días*, Navarra 1982, pp.142–6. On the indigenous martyrs and their extinct peoples see CIMI, *Outros 500. Construindo uma nova história*, São Paulo 2001, pp.203–41.
6. CNBB, *Por uma terra sem males. Fraternidade e povos indígenas*. Base text for the 2002 Brotherhood Campaign, São Paulo 2001, pp.31f.
7. CIMI, *Outros 500* (n.5), pp.157–65.
8. C. Nimuendaju Unkel, *As lendas da criação e destruição do mundo como fundamentos da religião dos apapocúva-guarani*, São Paulo 1987, pp.28f.
9. See P. Suess, *Weltweit artikuliert, kontextuell verwurzelt*. Theologie und Kirche Lateinamerikas vor den Herausforderungen des 'dritten Subjekts', Frankfurt 2001.
10. C. Lévi-Strauss, *Tristes tropiques*, here Port. trans. *Tristes trópicos*, Lisbon 1993, final chapter.

The Struggle for a Just Land Policy

TOMÁS BALDUINO

Since the Second Vatican Council and the 1968 Medellín Conference the general clamour of the peoples who live on the land in Brazil has echoed forcefully in the church, found a suitable response there, and been returned with redoubled force to the same people who, through their organizations, undertoook the heroic struggle for a just land policy. I propose to present this dramatic scenario from the 1970s to the present, but without detaching it from the earlier resistance by Indians, blacks and peasants from colonial times. I shall divide this complex whole into three aspects: (1) demands for land; (2) the church's response; and (3) rural organizations and the Landless Workers Movement.

I. Demands for land

Occupation of land has been, in practice, the one means used initially by the blacks and more recently by peasants in this continent-sized country in which title to land was, by the Lands Act of 1850, reserved exclusively to those who bought it. This was the means used to drive ex-slaves and the poor in general off the land. Then the military dictatorship, which ruled Brazil from 1964 to 1985, made a pact with the wealthy minority to modernize the country by offering them Amazonia. This was the most decisive move in favour of landowners, offering the major industries a rebate of half the taxes due in rent.

At the same time the governors of the states that legally comprise Amazonia put public lands up for sale for the furtherance of the cattle-ranching and timber trades. These were transactions made on a map, with no consideration of the fact that they involved lands inhabited by indigenous peoples from time immemorial and by families of settlers over recent decades. The new so-called owners of these lands were given *carte blanche* by the government to 'cleanse' the terrain of these occupants. Besides the private militias belonging to the new landowners, political support was provided to carry out this macabre operation. Santa Teresinha was a settlement founded by Dominican missionaries on the banks of the river Araguaia. It had a church, houses, a school, a health centre, small businesses, streets and squares. One fine day the owner of the Codeara Company arrived there and declared: 'You can take these buildings as you like, because this land is mine.'

Conflicts broke out on all sides, with violent expulsions, houses burned, crops destroyed, people imprisoned, tortured, and assassinated. The fact that crimes against rural workers went unpunished stimulated new rounds of assassinations, particularly of rural workers' leaders. Between 1985 and 1996, 976 rural workers were murdered. Only fourteen of those who had ordered these crimes were brought before the courts, and only seven were condemned. The government ordered the transfer of the indigenous Xavante people from their rich forest lands to an arid region, so as to benefit the Suía-Missu Company. Many of them died during the transportation process. Other Indian peoples succumbed to the brutal aggression brought about by the the construction of the Trans-Amazon highway, which was driven through their ancestral lands. Several black communities founded by runaway slaves were violently expelled, with police collaboration, to make way for huge ranches. Official policy bore heavily not only on the Indians and settlers of Amazonia but on the peasant population of the whole of Brazil. The military in effect decided that the country risked communist invasion from its countryside, and ferocioulsy repressed those who worked the land and those who supported them.

The pact between the government and the oligarchies made during the dictatorship is still in operation today. To take one example of what is causing huge indignation among the people: innumerable families are losing their lands when they are flooded by the building of huge hydro-electric plants, which are regularly handed over, through privatization, mostly to multinational corporations, who come to own the waters of the lakes created as well. The derisory monetary compensation is never sufficient for the expelled workers to buy other plots of land. Few escape destitution and hunger. The heroic popular organizations of those affected by dams are discriminated against and repudiated by the corporations and so watched and harshly repressed by the police. The same happens with the huge projects for reforestation with eucalyptus, vast soya plantations, and other monocultures that reinforce agribusiness, devastate the environment, and make family smallholdings impossible.

The headlong pursuit of profit by farmers has led to a rise in exploitation of labour, with a growing reduction in wages, creating – still today – slavery through debt on many farms in Amazonia. Farm labourers effectively reach farms already in debt for the price of the journey, which is refunded to them only when they arrive. Clothing, shoes, and medicines are sold to them exclusively by the farms. Several labourers have been shot trying to escape.

II. The church's response

One of the first churches to rebel against this iniquitous situation was that of São Féliz do Araguaia, in the person of its recently-consecrated bishop, Dom Pedro Casaldáliga. On 23 October 1971 he issued his pastoral letter 'A church in Amazonia in conflict with large estates and social marginalization'. This document was seen as a landmark, not only in the church but also throughout Brazilian society, for the reasoned, absolute condemnation it made, in passionate and prophetic tones, of the perverse, inhuman, and brutal side of the capitalism that rules in our country. This church of São Felix, so fragile in the face of the repression launched against it, which has only grown daily ever since, with threats, imprisonment, torture, court judgments, and murders not only of peasants and Indians but also of pastoral agents themselves, is a sign of what is happening to several churches in different parts of the country.

Other bishops issued clear, strong documents in 1973, such as 'I have heard the cry of my people', from the North East province, 'The exclusion of a people, or the cry of the churches', from the Centre West, and '*Y-juca pirama*' from the indigenous entity. The creation of the Pastoral Land Commission (CPT), informally linked to Brazilian National Bishops Conference (CNBB), was the means devised to bring together workers and agents spread and isolated throughout Brazil and at the same time to bring them support and hope in the midst of threats and repressions.

The CPT was born, then, from listening to the cries coming from the land and from the Samaritan campaign in defence of the fallen. The initial distinguishing feature of this service was not so much its ecclesial identity as its compassion. It was originally just the 'Land Commission', without the P for 'pastoral' in its title; the 'pastoral' was added later, logically in view of the religious origin of the initiative and also as a device for protection against military repression. Apart from this, its church provenance is not exclusively Catholic but ecumenical, as it has from the outset had the benefit of the courageous and admirable contribution made by members of the historical Protestant churches.

In one way the CPT brought something new to the church. This was its form of relating to the peasants who were suffering injustice. Faithful to the spirit of Medellín, put into practice in an exemplary manner by one of the greatest prelates of Latin America, Dom Leônidas Proaño, bishop of Rio Bamba in Ecuador, the CPT developed as a support agency for agricultural workers, recognizing and respecting in them their staus as subjects, authors, and addressees of their own history.

This fruitful intuition and new practice were officially backed by the CNBB in a document adopted by its eighteenth general assembly in 1980, 'The Church and Land Problems', where the following commitment appears (p.34): 'We reaffirm our support for the just initiatives and organizations of workers, placing our capabilities at the service of their cause. Our pastoral activity, while careful not to take the place of initiatives by the people, will stimulate careful and critical participation by workers in unions and associations, so that they can be truly autonomous and free social bodies, defending the rights and co-ordinating the claims of their whole class. And we support the efforts of land workers to bring about genuine agrarian reform.'

The CPT has been in existence for thirty years. In Bishop Casaldáliga's poetic expression, it has reached its 'Jubilee of dew and blood'. It has grown and matured throughout a dense and tense history of mistakes and achievements. It has taken on the faces of the most varied landscapes of Brazil in which it has found itself inserted. It has brought together lawyers, technologists, politicians, biblical scholars, and theologians in order to serve the people better. It has taken part in local pilgrimages, becoming inculturated in the religion of the people. It has also begun to be called 'Pastoral Commission for Land and Waters'. It has become a marker for church and society. It has joined with the National Forum for Agrarian Reform and Justice in the Countryside'. It has sought dialogue – not always easy – with church hierarchies, while preserving a healthy autonomy and a predominantly lay character.

In 2001 the CPT held its first Congress in the mystical and popular 'Grotto of the Good Jesus', a place where the poor go on pilgrimage, in the semi-arid area of Bahia, on the banks of the San Francisco River, which is threatened by death from privatization and pollution. By a decision of the CPT, working men and women made up two-thirds of the participants, with pastoral agents forming the other third. Perhaps surprisingly, these numbers of country people were unanimous in agreeing on the value and need for the CPT as 'a blessed instrument providing the essential support they still need today in the struggles for land and over land'.

III. Rural organizations and the Landless Workers Movement (MST)

An enlightening piece of information: from 18 to 22 April 2000, the Conference of the Indigenous Peoples of Brazil was held in Coroa Vermelha, Bahia. Its title was 'Indigenous, black, and popular resistence', and it brought together 3000 Indians, representing 170 peoples, most of them linked to one of ten indigenous organizations. In the end it was closed by the shock troops of the military police. It was notable for being the first gathering on such a scale in the whole history of the indigenous peoples of Brazil. Some of them were at war with each other just a few decades ago. One of the explanations given for this phenomenon is that CIMI (the Churches' Council for Missions to the Indians, formed in 1972) has encouraged and supported assemblies of tribal chiefs from different indigenous peoples, so that they could themselves see what their problems were and quite freely set about putting their own solutions in place.

Similarly, the base church communities, particularly in rural areas, began forming organizations of men and women to confront their local problems and needs. Spurred on by religious and biblical motivation, these groups developed a large degree of autonomy and a strong network of communications in their political quest for the solutions they sought. Many of the rural workers' organizations came from this birthplace. The CPT gave them considerable support. The workers then discovered the Agricultural Workers' Union. The early period of euphoria was followed by years of struggle and frustrations. The union structure was harnessed to the government and to the rural oligarchies. Union opposition then developed, attempting first to overturn the leadership from within but in the end turning against the whole structure of the union.

And what of the MST? The Minister for Rural Development, Raul Jungmann, has declared that there is a 'symbiosis between the MST and the CPT, the former being the executive arm of the CPT'. This view is also shared by some of the bishops. The fact of the matter is that the Brazilian élite finds it difficult to believe that peasants and Indians can think for themselves and walk on their own two feet.

Just as the CIMI has helped Indians to shoulder their status as agents of their history and has steadily stood by them and supported their organizations, so the CPT has done the same for rural workers, respecting them as protagonists of their struggles. The MST is not the only peasant organization in Brazil; it is, however, the largest and the oldest. It could be said to form the only consistent opposition to the present authoritarian government. The fact that it has survived in existence for seventeen years is a considerable victory in itself in view of the continual war the government has waged on it and compared to the periods earlier country workers' struggles lasted. It is truly a phenomenon regarded as a sign of hope today in Brazil and more widely in Latin America. It carries with it the same mystical liberative inspiration as the runaway slave settlement of Zumbi dos Palmares in the eighteenth century, or Antônio Conselheiro's Arraial de Canudos in the nineteenth, or the war of the 'Contestado do Beato José' or Julião's Peasant Leagues in the twentieth.[1]

The hope this movement inspires lies in the fact that it has been developed not through imposition by an organized vanguard but on the basis of the transformation that has surprisingly come about at the grassroots of the poor, largely through the popular education methods of Paulo Freire. To take just one example: the people of the north-eastern region, formerly humbly submissive to the factory owners, who were respected and venerated as companions and godfathers, have recently moved to occupy the cane plantations of these same proprietors in an organized fashion, transforming these private properties into a 'promised land' of consciousness and dignity, of productivity and sharing, of joy and celebration.

Conclusion

It is quite clear today that the current struggle for land, waged by numerous rural workers' organizations and closely linked to the Zapatista struggles of the Mexican Indians in Chiapas, is not aimed just at gaining a plot of ground on which each family can work and survive, through the means of agrarian and agricultural reform. It is rather a quest for *radical and urgent change* of the current free-market model, which prioritizes the market to the most serious detriment of the great mass of those excluded from it. This can only be achieved on the basis of solid alliances and effective co-ordination of planning on the national, continental, and global levels. Hence the great hopes these organizations place in the World Social Forum at Porto Alegre as a great occasion for putting forward proposals internationally, in the certainty that another world is possible.

On the same lines, it is worth recalling, finally, that these popular organizations in Latin America and especially in Brazil are also looking to Europe as a possible ally in their struggle for a global change. Unfortunately, European organizations with similar aims seem generally unable, despite their generosity, to move beyond a one-handed approach to the Third World. They have not succeeded in developing the sensitivity needed to understand the contribution being made above all by the poor of Latin America, aimed at nothing less than the integral liberation of all men and women of the planet. This is why the CMT, together with CIMI, is helping to organize the 'return mission' to the old continent, which we see as an essential ally in the quest for a change from the international disorder, the causes of which are to be found more in the First World. This is how we view the outreach of our solidarity with and support for those whom we regard and respect as subjects, agents, and addressees of the way of liberation.

Note

1. Antônio Conselheiro: born 1830 as Antônio Vicente Mendes Maciel, worked as a lawyer until his wife ran off with a soldier in 1860, when he became a wandering holy man, giving advice on various problems – hence the sobriquet 'counsellor'. Founded the town of Canudos, known as the 'mud-walled Troy', for Indians, ex-slaves, and others. Attacked by the military, it was eventually destroyed after a massive four-month seige, with the loss of 15,000 lives. Antônio died shortly before it surrendered.

   Francisco Julião, known as 'the agitator', lawyer and leader of Peasant Leagues from 1954, proclaimed that land reform had to be brought about 'by law or by force'. Exiled to Mexico in 1964, returned to Pernambuco from 1979 to 1987, exiled once more, died in 1999 (trans.).

Pastoral Strategy in the Brazilian Mega-Cities

I. X-ray of the mega-city

Brazil is undergoing a dramatic urbanization. In 1940, 30% of the population, which was then around 41,000,000, lived in cities, with 70% in the
countryside. By 1996, the urban population had risen to 123 million,
amounting to 79%, leaving just 21% in rural areas. The great metropolitan
regions account for between 45,000,000 and 50,00,000 inhabitants.

Urbanization does not progress blindly. Nor can it be seen as a by-
product of industrialization: it precedes it. Yet the city, which made
industrialization possible, is transformed under its impact. As technology
imposes new production methods, so the urban configuration is re-
fashioned, with psychic and physical effects on its inhabitants.

An X-ray of the city can be read in many ways. Signs of a robust and
vigorous organism allow the prognosis of a guaranteed future. The primary
evidence it provides is that the society of the future will live in cities. Their
power of attraction constantly seduces more and more people. This will be
my starting point. Nevertheless, cities show so many abnormal traits that the
analyst cannot appreciate them all from a single diagnosis. I have chosen to
single out two major features: decadence and violence. Three words, then,
sum up the results of the X-ray: seduction, decadence, and violence, each
with its consequences.[1]

1. Seduction with a pinch of illusion

The starting point for many people moving to cities is the search for work.
Capitalist mechanization and modernization of agriculture, the high cost of
borrowing, and the impossibility for small farmers to compete with agribusiness ranching have produced unemployment in the countryside, leading
the younger generations to go to the cities to seek work. Others dream of
earning higher wages, even if they could continue working in the bush. The
city stage has bright lights and its audience, drawn from so many places,

dazzles. The most seductive element is the feeling of freedom from the controls imposed by a small town, where rigid patterns apply, neighbours keep watch, and everyone knows everyone else. The city provides a vast anonymity, so people think they can be themselves, without the moral restraints imposed by rural society.

There are greater possibilities for work and for the children to study. As the importance of better education is increasingly realized, so the attraction of the city grows. It offers opportunities for cultural enhancement, from academic life to the artistic offerings of theatres, cinemas, and shows. Life in the bush progresses without novelty, monotonous and boring.[2] The city, on the other hand, looks like a box full of surprises and novelties, with its amusements and pleasure zones.

Well-being and comfort are taking on greater importance in today's valuation. The shop windows of cities display the latest products of technology, which promise satisfaction of many repressed desires. Life in the countryside looks increasingly harder, with its endless heavy work. So the attraction of the urban society of well-being, of pleasure, of consumption, with its more abundant offerings of material and cultural goods, becomes irresistible. Shopping malls, the cathedrals of consumer society, fascinate the curious gaze of recent arrivals from the interior or those who come to visit them. One can spend the whole day there without ceasing to be amazed. Health also tips the scales towards the city. There is access to better health facilities there, with better-equipped hospitals. Illnesses and problems that can easily lead to death in the countryside can be treated properly in the city.

The pinch of illusion and disappointment comes later. The city lights do not shine on everyone. The poor have no real access to this world. They can experience it only in desire and fantasy. And the farther the wonders of the shop windows recede, the more frustrated they feel. And moreover, the more people who migrate, the more urban conditions deteriorate, creating more and more peripheral slums. And decadence instead of the dream. Repression in place of realization.

2. Decadence

On any normal day, the great cities of Brazil have a population of adults and children living in the streets. There are now several generations who were born there and still live there, living under flyovers, in empty spaces.

The mega-cities have spawned a new type of worker: rubbish collectors.

They live on what the city throws out. They have decided to face this situation not just as a period of misfortune but as a possible stable way of life. So in greater Belo Horizonte ASMARE (the Association of Collectors of Paper, Cardboard, and Recyclable material) was organized more than fifty years ago, in order to take over this whole area of work, which had been carried out in an archaic and tolerated fashion. The rubbish collectors cut out the middlemen who bought the material from them and sold it on to recycling plants. Now they control the whole process from collection to sale. The city's rubbish has produced a new consciousness of struggle and organization.

But there is another side to this picture. The streets are being invaded by a growing army of excluded young people and adults working as prostitutes. A thousand devices, ranging from falsifying papers to bribing policemen, make a mockery of the law that forbids the solicitation of minors.

Whether as cause or as effect, economic and cultural poverty, aggravated by the prevailing new economic laws, pervades all these aspects. Unemployment is growing, as is the number of those suffering from diseases thought to have been eradicated. The failure of the preventative health-care system makes the situation worse. Those in work see their fixed wages decreasing in value, eaten away by low but constant inflation.

An immediate consequence is the increase in slum dwellings, the degrading of quality of life. Unplanned urban sprawl disorganizes the road system and public transport even more. It produces workers physically exhausted by the journey to work and back home. And the human crushes on transport lead to an increase in violence.

Urban living corrodes peoples' religious values and views from within. It cuts them off from their roots. It fixes them in the solitude of anonymity, which gnaws at their soul. It makes primary relationships more difficult by categorizing them. It takes so much of people's energies that they have none left for religious, artistic, or even leisure activities. Everything goes into work, travel, home. And in the family, relationships degenerate under the impact of media culture, which provides the only human palliative, while itself destroying people's interiority.

3. *Violence*

Jean Delumeau has written that it was not easy to get into Augsburg at night.[3] Fear came from outside, and the city defended itself with walls and drawbridges. Today fear comes from within the metropolis. One does not go to certain places at certain times. Secure space in the great cities is steadily being reduced, and during the hours of darkness it is virtually impossible to go out. Urban violence is dictating to people where they can go and when they can do so. It is increasingly limiting the basic right to come and go.

Umberto Eco has reproduced the apocalyptic hypothesis that R. Vacca conceived in a sort of imaginary guidebook, in a plausible succession of a huge traffic jam, the impossibility of finding air-traffic controllers to replace those stuck in the traffic, a plane crashing into a power line, causing a black-out in the city and appearance of hordes of vandals, who ransack everything they can find. The whole builds up in a terrible crescendo.[4] Well, there is no need to turn to any imagined succession of factors: a general strike by police in the city of Salvador de Bahia produced a similar situation, a real tropical St Bartholomew's Night. The sad outcome: six banks attacked, forty buses stoned, dozens of shops and their stocks sacked, hundreds of hooded men roaming the streets carrying firearms, some storming wildly through the alleys of a shopping complex terrorizing the shopkeepers, many of whom fled in fear while others came out armed prepared to defend themselves at gunpoint against possible attack, radio stations appealing to the population not to leave their houses, public transport reduced to a minimal service, a 60% increase in telephone calls as people enquired after the safety of relatives or friends, blocking the lines. The number of murders increased from the average of three in twenty-four hours to ten.

These figures are from the press. What do they show? That in a city considered one of the most tranquil it was enough for the news that it was unpoliced for a world of crime and frenzy to break out. This means that it is there and ready to explode at any moment. In fact, acts of violence are liable to be committed somewhere all the time. People live habitually with violence. Drugs have recently become a complicating and augmenting factor, bringing terrible crime in their wake. The frenzy and insecurity generated by violence has reached a point where our cities cannot offer safe conditions for hosting major international gatherings. When Rio de Janeiro hosted the Eco-summit in 1992, the Brazilian government brought the army out on to the streets and placed tanks in front of the shanty town of Rocinha. A show of police force brought peace for the few days of the summit, after which the city reverted to its daily violence.

Such an x-ray could be made of any major city.[5] Elements of it are in fact to found in all of them. Meanwhile, in the Third World, the deterioration of human life in the mega-cities is incomparably worse, and the corrective measures applied some time ago in the major cities of the First World are not being taken by anyone.

II. The church's pastoral strategy

Faced with this urban scene, what pastoral stategies has the church in Brazil evolved to respond to it? What responses has it proposed or carried out? I shall indicate two pastoral approaches, one of a charismatic persuasion, which plays a consolation role, and the other of a social nature, which keeps its critical bite.

1. Consolation

Although there have been spasmodic outbreaks of unrest in the mega-cities, there is still the question asked by Milton Santos, a nationally renowned geologist, who died recently. Why do they not explode?[6] He saw cities as having the capacity for producing a system of worked out actions and of encompassing structures in the socio-cultural world that work on citizens' mentality, disarming their explosive impulses, encouraging passive behaviour and thereby holding back tendencies to revolt.

These include the activities of many religions and sects that deaden unsatisfactions, turn peoples' minds away from them, and incite them to political passivity. One form of this is charismatic consolation, which acts as a tranquilizer. Obviously there are many other elements that contribute to this anaesthetizing therapy: sport, carnival, the beach, popular festivals, TV soaps, and so on. I shall examine the charismatic pastoral strategy only under its consolatory aspect, though it clearly has other sides that have the potential to effect structural change in the church.

One fact is clear. Regular, traditional religious observance declines from the moment when people leave a rural society in which the enormous weight of tradition impelled them to follow a religious routine. Habits kept up by the environment counted for more than personal convictions. In the big cities, there is a lack of stimulus from the surrounding culture. Gradually, practice becomes rare and disappears.

Various recent researches into the religious practices of the population and the presence of the Catholic Church point to apparently contradictory evidence. The religions, as institutions, are losing their power to define truths and practices that people accept docilely. People are becoming increasingly free and independent when faced with such prescriptions. The dogmatic teachings and moral precepts of the church are followed by a minority of those who call themselves Catholics. On the issue of contraceptives, 73% of Catholics do not accept the official teaching of the church.[7]

There is, nonetheless, evidence of recognition of the social and political relevance, especially of the Catholic Church, as an institution within the body of society. This is confirmed by the result of research carried out by IBOPE in 1990, which made the Catholic Church the most trusted institution in public opinion, with a 78% rating, far above radio, which came second with 58%.[8] More recently, in another research project carried out by the journal *Imprensa* among 1,605 young people in the five major Brazilian state capitals, most of them replied that the Catholic Church was the most trustworthy institution, with the papers second and the Protestant churches third.

Besides the public presence of the church, there is also intense personal religious feeling. Research carried out by CERIS, an organ of the bishops' conference, showed the great majority of those interviewed giving their reasons as personal fulfillment and a search for ethics, experience of God, and existential quest, though there was still a minority of between 17% and 27% who cited tradition. This reveals a religious thirst. In certain situations, this is enlivened by the harsh conditions of city life. This is just the point at which consolation pastoral strategy comes in.

There is a pastoral presence that offers the sacramentary rites and other forms of traditional piety in response to the requirements of people who hold on to their traditional religious views in the city. It is somewhat in decline but still has weight, thanks to the powers of resistance shown by old religious archetypes. This keeps many traditional pastoral practices alive, in the Catholic Church and others. It is the consolation of the traditional.

The novelty comes from the charismatic and Pentecostal side. In many local churches the Catholic Church has recently developed an intense charismatic pastoral strategy, associated with techniques drawn from the media. This reaches both the two main socio-cultural strata of society. With the poorer classess, the charismatic approach is successful in conveying a new sense of life and of struggle on people suffering on account of their material poverty, unemployment, alcohol addiction, broken homes, or spiritual despair. Some of these seek direct and immediate solutions to their material and/or spiritual problems and attribute any alleviation or resolution to the action of the Holy Spirit. The better-off economically are looking for a spiritual meaning to life. Consumerism, wealth, worldliness, or hedonism no longer satisfy their desires. They are on the lookout for religious experiences that will bring them inner peace.

This pastoral approach combines mass celebrations with small prayer groups. It is distinguished by its use of music and festivity, in long celebrations full of euphoria, gestures, invocations, mantras, repeated Alleluias and Amens. These produce radical conversions, often associated with rites of exorcism and healing of physical, psychic, and spiritual ailments. The celebrations appeal through the symbolic aesthetics of their setting and by their music, so that people feel at home in them. These churches transmit their celebrations through the media. In Brazil they now own several television channels with near national coverage. They reach millions through buying slots on the main commercial channels and by placements in TV soaps and documentaries.

2. The social side

Besides the charismatic strategy, the church in Brazil is predominantly preocupied with the social question. This is where it invests the best and most original aspects of its strategy.

It has seen the ambiguity of consolation pastoral care from the outset. It has also seen that other churches, particularly the Universal Church of the Kingdom of God, are unbeatable at this type of witness. It knows that there is no sense in trying to compete with them, which would be neither evangelical nor practical.[9] In a country with extreme needs in the fields of health, of education, of the minimum requirements for life, the church has deliberately set out to contribute emergency charitable pastoral programmes. It puts out the fires, knowing that it cannot extinguish their causes. Such a course has long been part of the church's tradition. There is nothing new in this.

The originality comes in the process of consciousness-raising associated with immediate and charitable help. When the church gives aid, it undertakes a task of political education with families in need. This has happened especially with the upbringing of children, which became so prominent that the Brazilian government has adopted many of its practices, especially the provision of home-made milk products and education in hygiene for mothers with babies. In the free-market economy, where giants win and powerful, globalized corporations making the most of the latest in information technology rule, the pygmies of the informal sector are devoured unless they can come up with a minimum of organization. The church has devoted itself to encouraging a people's community economy. A part of special collections has helped to start programmes in this area.

On the national level, the church has evolved significant socio-political initiatives. Seven years ago it promoted, together with other organizations in civil society, the 'Cry of the excluded' on the occasion of the National Day. When the nation commemorates its independence, the church, through demonstrations in the principal cities, denounces the fact that so many people are excluded from the mainstream of the country's life. In 2001 it gathered crowds estimated at hundreds of thousands, and this event is now being copied in other Latin American countries. Last year the 'Cry of the excluded' was linked with a campaign against corruption, demanding the establishment of a Parliamentary Commission of Inquiry to investigate corruption in various governing bodies. From 2 to 7 September 2000, in an effort to alert the national consciousness to the grave consequences of and the obscurity surrounding the country's external and internal debt, the Catholic Church and other groups sponsored a 'National Plebiscite on External Debt', in which electors were asked whether they approved of the agreement reached with the IMF, whether they thought it right to continue paying the external debt without a public inquiry into the matter, and whether internal debt to speculators shoud be paid out of the public purse. The first question was answered in the negative by 93.6% of those who voted, and the other two by over 95%. These are signs of the church's pastoral presence in society to a notable extent.

The 'Brotherhood Campaign' is another indication of the church's presence in society. Since 1964, a Lent pastoral campaign has been organized around a basic theme, usually of a social nature. In 2001 this was the drug problem, with the motto 'Life, Yes; Drugs, No'. Other campaign subjects have been the land question, homeless children, black people, social communication, women, the world of work, young people, the housing question, the family, the excluded, politics, prisoners, unemployment, human dignity and peace, and so on. Pastoral work with various categories of the excluded includes concern for prisons, for shanty towns, for marginalized women, for rubbish collectors, for street children, for the black and indigenous populations. With the growing problems of drug and alcohol abuse, a sobriety campaign on preventative therapeutic lines has been developed.

Running through various social pastoral schemes is the network of base church communities (CEBs), nourished on a popular spirituality, especially in the biblical circles. These are organized on the basis of the exegetical method developed by Friar Carlos Mesters.[10] Their originality lies chiefly in the linkage between the word of God and life, between faith and the situation. They are based on the triplet: text, pre-text, context – the text of scripture, read in the social setting of life (pre-text) and of the community's faith (context). The circles make use of major events in the church's life in the choice of theme. Several decades ago, September was chosen as Bible month. Each year a book of the Bible is chosen and programmes are prepared for the biblical circles. The same applies to the Brotherhood Campaign, Christmas novenas, and many other occasions.

The base communities and circles work best in the shanty towns around the cities. The middle classes prefer prayer groups with a more charismatic character.

Conclusion

A public presence, the social question, a network of communities woven into the social fabric with a critical voice, and a growing awareness of the Spirit-centred charismatic phenomenon have been the pastoral concerns of the Catholic Church in Brazil at the beginning of this millennium. From these it has drawn sap to reinvigorate its internal structures, suffering, at this time, from the tension between institutional reinforcement and an attitude of openness to the complex problems of the modern and the post-modern city.

Notes

1. J. B. Libanio, *As lógicas da cidade. O impacto sobre a fé e sob impacto da fé*, São Paulo 2001.

2. J. Comblin, *Viver na cidade. Pistas para a pastoral urbana*, São Paulo 1996, pp.7ff.

3. J. Delumeau, *Sin and Fear: The Emergence of Western Guilt Culture, 1300–1800*, New York, [2]1991.

4. U. Eco, *Viagem na irrealidade cotidiana*, Rio [3]1984, pp.75ff.

5. G. della Pergola, *Viver a Cidade. Orientações sobre problemas urbanos*, São Paulo 2000

6. M. Santos, 'A metrópole: modernização, involução e segmentação' in L. Valladares & E. Preteceille, *Reestruturação Urbana, Tendências e desafios*, São Paulo 1990, p.189.

7. CERIS, *Tendências Atuais do Catolicismo no Brasil*, Rio 2000: research carried out among E, D, and C social classes in the country's six main cities.

8. A. Antoniazzi, 'Pesquisa de opinião sobre religiões na Grande BH' in *Construir a Esperança*, Archdiocese of Belo Horizonte (March/9, n. 3), p.4.

9. J. Edênio dos Reis Valle, 'A "Universal": um fenômeno mercadológico-religioso brasileiro' in *REB* 58 (1998) no. 230, pp.350–84.

10. C. Mesters. *Círculos Bíblicos*, Petrópolis 1973; idem, *Por trás das palavras*, Petrópolis ⁴1980; idem, *Flor sem defesa*, Petrópolis 1983; Eng. trans. *Defenseless Flower: A New Reading of the Bible*. Maryknoll, NY 1989.

Shifts in Theology; Socio-Ecclesiastical Changes: Recent Developments in Theology in Brazil

CARLOS PALACIO

Speaking of 'theology in Brazil' in such a short compass and in such general terms is a risk that can be taken only within the bounds of the original proposal for this issue of *Concilium* dedicated to Brazil: to provide 'news' of this country, making its human and religious vitality more widely known. What does this imply in the case of theology?

It would be exceedingly pretentious to try to provide a *panorama* of theology in Brazil here, since theology cannot be reduced to either Catholic or dogmatic theology. To do this, I should have to provide partial accounts of what is happening in Protestant theology, or in other areas such as biblical exegesis. None of this will be found here. This will be simply a 'summary account' of what has happened in Catholic theology in Brazil over the last decades, taking the part for the whole, following that inveterate habit of identifying Brazil and Catholicism (which seems to have spread to the planning of this volume!). And yet it is not unreasonable to speak of 'theology in Brazil', since many of the questions raised here are 'ecumenical' and apply beyond confessional boundaries.

Theology in Brazil cannot be separated from the major factor represented by liberation theology or from the names of its most eminent and best known exponents. This observation helps to limit what is understood as 'recent developments'. Effectively, this means in the last three decades, of which the first two, the 1970s and 1980s, coincide with the genesis and the apogee of liberation theology. The third, the 1990s, is when one can really see other new tendencies and directions, which are, strictly speaking, 'recent' developments.

This, then, is the outline of this rapid tour of these developments: a brief summary of what the 1970s and 1980s meant, some features of the new situation that came about in the 1990s, and some interpretative comments to conclude.

I. The golden age: the 1970s and 1980s

This extraordinary period can be understood only within the ecclesial and social context immediately preceding it. In the church, these were the immediate post-conciliar years, a true springtime for the church, the dynamism of which was prolonged by the General Assembly of the Latin American bishops at Medellín in 1968 and by the onset of a 'new understanding' of the church in Latin America. The Brazilian church undoubtedly played a particularly prominent role in this process. Through a series of convergent circumstances, the Brazilian episcopate was the launch pad for this 'ecclesial about-turn', in Brazil itself and the rest of Latin America.

On the social side, this was a period shot through with contradictions. Besides a situation of extreme poverty that was tearing the social fabric apart, a growing number of Christian leaders came to realize that this situation was a profound contradiction of faith in Jesus Christ. Apart from this, the revolutionary climate seemed to bring the suppression of this structural imbalance within grasp. The utopia of socialism was nourishing the dream of a new society. It was just in this context that the long and dark night of military rule fell on Brazil – and on most of the continent.

Brazilian theology would be incomprehensible outside these circumstances, since it was above all a response to the *vital need* to reflect theologically on the living, actual situation of the church community. This experience was at one and the same time *experience of God* and responsibility for transforming the *human and social situation*. It was both critical understanding of the social situation and spiritual experience of conversion to the God of Jesus Christ in the poor.

The 'natural home' of theology was church commnity life identified with the poor. This is what explains many of the characteristics of this theology: the fact that it is reflection called forth by reality, that it does not separate theology from life, that it forms close links between theology and the people. It was no accident that theology sought to appear more 'pastoral' and less 'academic', tied in with popular movements and open to the challenges posed by the pastoral situation. This is what also explains the close ties between theology and the religious life, not just the fact that quite a few theologians were members of religious orders but above all the significance of what was called 'insertion', that great exodus from 'religious life' to the places where most of the people actually lived.

This theology did not seek its sources primarily in traditional treatises; its subjects came to it from life itself. One has only to cast an eye over the publications of the time to see that social and spiritual, political and religious themes are intertwined in them in a passionate quest for a living synthesis. At this period the question of method was worked out, and an ecclesiology and christology developed in an endeavour to shed light on the new situation of the faith. In the 1980s – and impelled by external factors such as increasing Vatican distrust – liberation theologians felt compelled to compile a sort of coherent 'doctrinal *corpus*'. The well known series 'Teologia e Libertaçao' ['Liberation and Theology' in the UK edition] included several of the classical subjects of theology, studied from the viewpoint of liberation theology. The value of this endeavour was to show that it was possible to give an account in orthodox style to the whole content of Christian faith within the perspective of liberation theology.[1]

It was in these years that Brazilian theology acquired its distinctive features. These were the years of its greatest creativity and those that saw the arrival of a generation of theologians who were to leave their mark on theological reflection over many years. This is not the place to list them.[2] What matters is the fact itself: the onset of a new way of 'doing theology'. The greatest contribution liberation theology and theology in Brazil have made to the universal church is the fact of having existed. And this was a new event: for the first time, after many centuries of ecclesial uniformity, one particular church asserted itself as not just a mirror-image of the 'universal church' but as the source of its own original experience, which, because of being this, required a theological reflection capable of interpreting this life of its own and so, also in its own way, of being creative and not mere repetition of a 'universal theology'.

This event lies behind what seems obvious to us today: the existence of other *contextual theologies* – such as those of Asia and Africa – proper to *particular churches* that are claiming their full recognition so that they can take inculturation of the faith and the gospel seriously. In this sense, it was a pioneering and paradigmatic event. For the church in Brazil, nevertheless, it involved a long and painful *via crucis*. But it was by 'going through death' that this achievement could become a prophetic sign for the universal church. The realization that the 'option for the poor' formed part of the church's message and mission, and the need to live and think the faith *from* the special circumstances of each church, are today an integral part of the self-understanding of the universal church.

II. The 1990s: a time of waiting?

The panorama of theology in Brazil changed as the situation of the church in the country was modified. The first signs of change were already making themselves felt at the end of the 1980s. The situation was different, in both the social and the ecclesial spheres. The self-understanding of the church in Brazil no longer provided a common basis for theology. In part this was due to the disconcerting evolution of the universal church after Vatican II, and in part also to the internal changes within the episcopate and among the Christian faithful.

The state of society also changed, but not in the direction hoped for. The utopia of a just society evaporated; the globalization of the economy aggravated social inequalities and poverty; modernity confused traditional values and wove a new social fabric in its own image: individuals and groups, rich and poor. And the bishops found themselves puzzled, not to say disorientated, when faced with this situation.

In these circumstances it is understandable that theology should discreetly have set its sights on other matters. Suffice to glance at the publications of these years or note the subjects dealt with in the latest SOTER (Society for Theology and Religious Studies) Congresses to appreciate the deep shifts that have affected theology: the appeal of sacred and religious realms in present-day society; inter-religious dialogue; new paradigms; challenges arising from minorities such as the blacks or the Indians and from women; then again problems posed by ecology, bio-ethics, and so on.

A retrospective look over the past ten or fifteen years will show that they marked the beginning of a new stage of theology in Brazil, one that is inseparable from a new way of being church in a different social, cultural, and religious context. The question is to know how to interpret this stage. Is it a time of waiting, or has the whole agenda shifted?

What does this new stage look like? Its appearance is not very distinct, but there are some indicators that allow us to sketch its profile. The most immediate and obvious feature is the shift of place, the move from the actual life of the community to 'academia'. This shift brings with it an inevitable fragmentation of theology – of its concerns, its outlooks, its approaches. Theology seems to be distancing itself from life and becoming more theoretical. What is the evidence for this perception?

The most visible aspect of this change is what one might call a *concentration on the institutional*. Until a few years ago there were only three pontifical faculties in Brazil with the authority to confer academic degrees: the FAI in São Paulo, the CES (Centre of Higher Studies) in Belo Horizonte and the PUC (Pontifical Catholic University) in Rio. In the last decade theology has increasingly migrated to university circles, either incorporating former institutes of theology or even seminary courses into Catholic universities (as, for example, with PUC-RS – Pontifical Catholic University of Rio Grande do Sul – or the Catholic University of Gioânia), or forming itself into a university centre (such as UniFAI – Assumption University Centre – in São Paulo), or again creating new institutes (such as ISTA in Belo Horizonte, the new Franciscan Theology Institute in Petrópolis, and numerous other institutes spread around the country, including ITESP in São Paulo and ITESC in Florianópolis, to name but two).

This phenomenon might mean that theological training is a pressing option for theology at the present time, with major repercussions in the creation of a theologically literate laity, vital for the non-clerical church of the future. But resources – material and human – will affect the quality of teaching, which cannot be automatically guaranteed or taken for granted. In this sense, the multiplication of centres might be a threat to teaching quality and to research.

The second aspect of this change is the establishment of post-graduate courses in *religious studies* (as at the Federal University of Juiz de Fora, or the Pontifical Catholic University of São Paulo, or the Methodist University of São Bernardo-SP). The phenomenon is relatively recent and would require a deeper study of the status of theology, which is not the same thing as modern 'religious studies'. Without this prior clarification, there will inevitably be an air of ambiguity hanging over a dialogue that is not only fruitful but necessary. This ambiguity might have been present at the formation in 1985 of SOTER itself, as its name, embracing both theology and religious studies, implies.

The third and final aspect is the prospect of the possibility of the state giving *official recognition* to faculties of theology. This is a new aspect, and as important as it is imponderable. It is important for dialogue and the common construction of meaning in a secular society, but it is imponderable because it is impossible to foresee what repercussions it would have on the pattern of theology. (Some centres have already been recognized: the Lutheran Higher School of Theology in São Leopoldo, the Methodist Institute of Religious Sciences in São Bernardo, and the Theological Institute of Taubaté.)

III. How to interpret this new situation in theology?

Without making any claim to make a definitive reading of this development
it is possible to suggest some lines along which we can better understand this
transitional phase.

1. The shifts of theology in Brazil have left theology in a state of deep
vulnerability. It is suffering a double orphanhood: ecclesial and social.
Theology has been orphaned by a church which has left itself open to the
most varied and even contradictory choices. Such fragmentation can only
leave theology confused. How can it 'think' church life when the experience
of communities is so diverse? On the other hand, this very diversity is the
result of the giddy pace of social and cultural change in society, so it is
not surprising that the church should not know exactly what its place is in
society or how to carry out its function.

2. The encounter between theology and the modern mentality is one of
the elements accounting for this vulnerability of theology. It comes about in,
for example, taking on the analyses made by social sciences or in dialogue
with religious studies. Now modern reasoning is a *secular* and *fragmentating*
process; that is, it situates the 'objects' it examines in a framework of
immanence, thereby working a reduction of meaning. In its encounter with
this reasoning process, theology can be affected by this reductionist temptation. Theological reasoning is truly theological only when it takes an
overview of the whole of reality and subjects it to the logic of faith. If
theology abdicates from its own rationality it will end up getting lost in the
same logic as modern reasoning. Is this not the impression theology sometimes gives when it stoops, with no other resources, over such 'fragments'
of modern precoccupations as the so-called social minorities, feminism, or
religious phenomenology?[3]

3. Theology's move towards the academic sphere should be viewed with
clarity. This is not the first time in its history that theology has faced this
problem, and ways of resolving it have not always been peaceful. From the
Middle Ages to the present, with the experience of the 'expulsion' of theology from university curricula in modern times, theology should have
learned a lot from the marks left by this history, which still affect it today.
This is not just a question of its physical setting. It seems undeniable that, in
a pluralistic society, theology has an important part to play in a common
'construction of meaning'. The question is knowing whether universities, as
they have been conceived by modern theories, are the right place for con-
structing meaning at the present time.

The analysis sketched here does not claim to be an exhaustive interpretation of this phase of transition or waiting for theology in Brazil. The lines put forward here should be enough to give some idea of what is at stake in this development. Everything suggests that theology in Brazil will recover its 'own special' face – which has been its most original characteristic – only when it becomes capable of embracing all these new challenges in its own way of thinking the faith.

Notes

1. For general information, besides the individual volumes in this series (of which twelve only of the originally planned fifty-four were published in English: *trans.*) there is the useful collective work ed. I. Ellacuría and J. Sobrino, *Mysterium Liberationis. Fundamental Concepts of Liberation Theology*, Maryknoll, NY, 1993.

2. For more detailed information on authors and publications see J. B. Libânio and A. Antoniazzi, *20 anos de teologia na América Latina e no Brasil*, Petrópolis 1994.

3. One indication of this new way of approaching the modern mentality is the distance that separates two basic works by C. Boff: *Teologia e prática. A teologia do político e suas mediações*, Petrópolis 1977, and *Teoria do método teológico*, Petrópolis 1998.

The Contribution of Brazilian Ecclesiology to the Universal Church

Some years ago J.-B. Metz said that present-day Christianity is a Third World religion that once had its origins in the First World. It is a fact that over half the world's Catholics live in the Third World, 42.35% in Latin America, of which 32% are in Brazil. These figures do not just signify quantity but involve a new quality of being church that is increasingly worthy of consideration. As colonized peoples, we were born as a mirror-Christianity of European Christianity. Rites, doctrines and institutions were transplanted from there to here. But after five hundred years we can say that we are slowly changing into a source-Christianity, with our own particular ecclesial experiences that demonstrate the rooting of the Christian faith in the new peoples that are coming into being here. A dark-faced Christianity is being born, a new Christianity of the tropics. In this sense, the Brazilian experience is interesting for the promises it contains.

What contribution can the Brazilian ecclesial experience offer to the universal church? I shall here restrict my observations to just a few points.

I. Discovery of the sub-world

The Second Vatican Council succeeded in opening the church to the modern world, becoming reconciled to its achievements, particularly in the realms of technology and science. But it did not concentrate sufficiently on the drama of the great masses of humanity, victims of the modern world.

The Brazilian church gave an original reception to Vatican II where the situation of poverty and destitution were concerned. It realized that there is not just a modern world with its development but also a sub-world with its sub-development. These are not parallel realities. There are causal connections between the two which mean that sub-development is a sub-product of the type of development the wealthy nations have created for themselves.

This generates great wealth on one side *at the cost of* impoverishment of the other. This sub-development means suffering for millions of people. Analytically, it means political and social oppression. Theologically, it means social and structural sin. The solution lies in breaking the development/sub-development connection through a process of liberation through which the country held in sub-development makes a journey of development for itself and for the benefit of its own population.

II. Marriage between the church and the poor

It is important to stress that the commitment of the church to the poor did not stem from a left-wing ideology or from the influence of Marxist ideas about the revolution that was needed. It was born out of com-passion shown by Christian pastors and faithful in the face of the suffering and passion of the people. They experienced what Jesus did: *miserior super turbas*. The fact of being born out of an evangelical and mystical experience makes it indestructible, however much it is defamed by those in power and mis-understood by other brothers in faith who, from the Vatican and with the Vatican, try to empty it of content or spiritualize it.

What is hidden behind the option for the poor? Two extremely original visions are hidden. The first is that the poor are not just poor; they have a power of utopia, in thought and action; they are historical agents; they are capable, together with others, of transforming the perverse society under which we are suffering. This vision goes against the grain of the historical 'charity' of churches working *for* the poor but never *with* the poor and *from* the viewpoint of the poor. The second vision affirms that the poor, the great majority of whom are Christian, are helping to establish a new model of church, more rooted in people's daily lives, more committed to justice, organized more around forms of community and participation than of hierarchization and subordination.

This means that the poor can be active participants in society and in the church. The church in Brazil has delivered this vote of confidence in the poor and, in its basic options, has kept this confidence till today. When, in the history of Christianity, have the poor been accorded such a central place? They decide on whether the actions of the church, especially of its hierarchy, are in accordance with the gospel or not.

III. The re-invention of society and of the church

The option for the poor and for liberation has plunged the church into the Brazilian social process, which is highly dynamic and creative. As a national institution, it brings together all social levels, classes and groups. History has rarely produced examples of an institution that is conservative by nature and easily adapted to the status quo becoming prophetic and promoting actions designed to transform society. This has been the case with the church in Brazil, particularly through the National Conference of Bishops, which clearly opposed the military dictatorship and engaged in building a bottom-up, people's and participatory democracy. It has continued to organize specific actions by Christians over the whole country: by the peoples – indigenous and settlers – living in the jungle, by rural movements, by movements of the landless and the homeless, by blacks, by women, by street children, by those living in the shanty towns around the great cities, by workers' associations in the industrialized areas, by intellectuals working in universities and research institutes.

Like a table, four legs hold up this re-invention of the church and society.

The first is the people's re-appropriation of the word of God. They have learned to read the Bible, in its text, context and pretext, and to see themselves as the continuation of the biblical People of God. This has given birth to almost a million Bible-study groups, spread throughout every corner of this huge country. Reading the word in community, the people have learned to interpret the history in which the God of life is always on the side of those who have least life. They have learned to criticize society and also the church itself, with its lack of communion and sharing. More fundamentally, they have learned to dream of another type of world and society, not only for themselves but for all human beings.

The second leg is made up of the base church communities (CEBs), which now number around a hundred thousand over the whole country. These are not parish instruments for reaching out to the poor. They are an entire church, with resources of word, sacrament, structure and mission, at grassroots level. This is to say that the poor, abandoned by the institutional church, began to meet, first around the word and then, bringing several Bible-study groups together, beginning to form small communities. They embody the true definition of the church, as a community of the faithful. They are bringing about a new way of being church, characterized by communion and sharing. Ministries and services arise, and leadership is collegial and taken in turn. In place of formal rites, life as a whole is celebrated, expressed in rich symbolism typical of popular culture. A type of church with the face of the people is emerging, one that adopts the culture of the poor and incorporates the dreams of new men and women of another type of society in which human beings can deal humanly with one another and welcome each other as brothers and sisters.

The third leg is made up of social pastorals. The church becomes part of the struggles of the people and develops its own struggles, stemming from its own ecclesial engagement: movements for the landless, the homeless, Indians, blacks, human rights, street children, community health, popular art and culture . . . The social pastorals make the church part of the social conflict. They have managed to avoid two types of reductionism, both known and discussed here before Paul VI described them with great clarity in *Evangelii nuntiandi* (1975, nos. 32 and 34): religious reductionism and political reductionism. The church mission cannot be reduced to the religious field, as if it were detached from the temporal problems of society; neither can it be reduced to the political field, as if its task were to present a saving political programme. Its mission is to evangelize, which embraces both religious and political aspects: religious, through word, sacrament, and the formation of communities; political, through ethical commitment to social justice, to threatened life and to peace. The church speaks evangelically and not politically about politics; it speaks ethically and not politically about the dignity of the poor and their struggles for life and the means to life.

The fourth foot is liberation theology. Reflecting on the church's practices so as to deepen them, correct them and legitimize them, done in community and in communion with pastors, is called liberation theology. It is the theology embedded in the social pastorals and in the minds of the members of the base communities and of local churches that take the option for the poor seriously. It underlies, even if it not named as such, the principal documents of the Brazilan Bishops Conference. In Brazil this form of theology has always been dominant, as being the most adequate means of linking the discourse of faith with the discourse of poverty.

The result sought by these practices, together with corresponding reflection on them, is to re-discover the church in the midst of the great majority who are poor and to re-discover a new play of more egalitarian and just social relationships.

IV. Redeeming the terms *communio* and *populus Dei*

It is safe to say that nowhere in the universal church have the terms *communio* and *populus Dei* acquired such importance as in the development of the church in Brazil. The term *communio* is central to theology. By this, we understand the dynamic of the Holy Trinity, the mystery of creation in its relationship with the Creator, the incarnation of the Son, the indwelling of the Spirit, the relationships among Christians and even the pan-relationship of everything in the universe. Here one is speaking of communion without qualification. Any addition to it, as in *hierarchica communion*, for example, destroys the original sense of communion and projects an ideology justifying the actual situation within the church, composed of unequal relationships and subordination. The communion that finds its icon and source of inspiration in the Trinity ('the Holy Trinity is the best community', as the members of the base communities declare) does not tolerate inequalities or impositions of uniformity; instead, it starts from the differences that, through *communio* among all, create unity in diversity, a dynamic unity that is always open to new expressions. The concept of *communio* lies at the root of the ecclesiology of the base church communities and of their understanding of community ministries and services.

The other term that has been redeemed is 'People of God', placed by Vatican II before the hierarchical structure of the church. In no other church has there been such insistence on the church as people of God as in the self-understanding, practice and documents of the church in Brazil. This is not one metaphor for the church among many. It is a real description of what the church really is. But we need to understand the term properly: a people cannot exist on its own. It comes into being from linking the many communities that have worked out an understanding of community for themselves, created a common project of communion and sharing, and produced the practices through which to implement it. The people is the product of this linking process. For the church to be the people of God, it needs in the first place to be a people, which is not entirely evident. It forms itself into a people to the extent that it creates Christian communities and movements that, linked together, give rise to the people. This people then makes itself, through faith and the gospel, the people of God. It chooses God and feels itself called by God. What we have in the current model of the hierarchical church is not a people of God, but a mass of faithful, brought together in a chapel or a parish and subject to a hierarchy that alone commands word, sacrament, and leadership of the community.

The base church communities and the social pastorals are the matter that gives concrete form to the people of God, a phenomenon that can be observed sociologically at work within the social development of Brazil.

V. The universal relevance of the Brazilian church model

In Brazil, another way of being church has been shown to be possible. We are not condemned to go till the last judgment with the traditional model, which has produced so many structural tensions and conflicts through being, from its beginning, a source of inequalities and deficiencies in communion and in sharing. Our way carries on the great tradition, builds unity in its own way, and is more attuned to the perennial desires of men and women, to be subjects and not spectators of their own secular and sacred history. In this way the Brazilian experiment encourages Christians to hope that we can have a different and a better future. This is not only possible. Among us, it has become a palpable reality, charged with values and promises for ourselves and for so many others who are pursuing the same quest.

III. Future Demands and Challenges for Being Church in Brazil

The Globalization of Continental Challenges: A Call from Brazil on Understanding the Christian Faith

AGENOR BRIGHENTI

Historically, the church in Europe saw itself challenged by *modernity*; in Latin America by *poverty*; in Africa by *cultural pluralism*; in Asia by *religious pluralism*. Gustavo Gutiérrez pertinently remarked recently, at a colloquy held to mark the 575th anniversary of the founding of the Catholic University of Louvain, that today, with the emergence of a planet-wide consciousness and a globalized world, the various challenges that faced the different continents have become common to all. In effect, modernity is present and in crisis everywhere; the great religions cross all continents; the rescue of autochthonous cultures is a widespread imperative; poverty is present also in the First World. While these challenges are present in different ways on each continent, and in each of the countries within them, the fact is that they impose a hermeneutical task on the Christian faith as such, regardless of the variety of contexts in which they are embodied. Brazil finds itself inserted into this planet-wide context.

I. The challenge of rationality

There is no denying that the thrust of modern civilization has brought about a Copernican revolution in the sphere of rationality. Christianity in its second millennium resisted for five centuries before opening itself to a world that had been gestated, to a large extent, outside the church and against it, yet founded on gospel values. From the first half of the last century, the church in Europe had to embark on the arduous task of understanding the faith in the new context. It based this mainly on the First Enlightenment – the emancipation of the individual subject and of subjective reasoning. Later, the so-called 'genitive theologies' (political theology, theology of revolution, theology of earthy realities, theology of hope, and so on), and especially the theology of liberation in Latin America, worked out a hermeneutic of faith on the basis of the Second Enlightenment – the emancipation of social subjects and of practical reasoning.

1. Modernity in crisis

Meanwhile, there are deep transformations in progress, not only in developed societies that are in the 'post' phase – post-industrialized, post-Christian, post-modern – but also in Third World countries such as Brazil, in which pre-modern, modern, and post-modern exist alongside each other. The turn of the millennium undoubtedly coincides with a time in which we have the feeling that 'everything that is solid is coming apart in the air' (Jean Baudrillard). In the wake of the 'crisis of modernity', which many have characterized as an 'epochal change' or a 'crisis of civilization', we have the crisis of 'technical-instrumental reasoning' (Frankfurt School), followed by the crisis of 'meta-narratives' based on 'cold reason that ignores the heart's reasons' (emotional reasoning). 'Light thinking' or 'the culture of the vacuum', in the apt phrases of Gianni Vattimo and Gilles Lipovestsky, beckon as the only form of reason – 'weak reason'. The sciences in general, which in the last century were 'much closer to power than to truth' (Pedro Demo), are in a full 'crisis of paradigms'. The great social ideas, which aimed at bringing about revolutions, have finished as 'disenchantment with utopias' (Herbert Marcuse) and seem to point to 'the end of history' (Francis Fukuyama). We are left with the bitter taste of the present, the 'triumph of the solitary individual' (J. I. González-Faus). Technology, apparently the only sector to have triumphed, is nevertheless responsible for a sick planet, in which 'human life and its ecosystenms' (Leonardo Boff) are threatened. We are all in the grip of a 'feeling of orphanhood', marked by instability, insecurity, and, in many cases, fear and apocalypticism.

2. The gestation of a Third Enlightenment

The great question emerging from the midst of so much ambiguity is, though, whether modernity has in fact run its course. The tensions present at the heart of so-called post-modernity suggest that it has not. As Jurgen Habermas and A. Tourraine have wisely warned, the present 'crisis of modernity' is far from being the demise of this 'civilizational project'. We are rather faced with the challenge of a 'super-modernity', in which the First and Second Enlightenments have to be complemented by a Third Enlightenment – the emancipation of otherness as gift or of communicational reasoning. There is everywhere an explosion of serious investigation of the 'other' as a horizon of meaning, the way to 'the great Other' (Lévinas), or Absolute, the true subject of ethics (Wittgenstein), absent from the main spheres of present-day social life.

3. The challenge for understanding of the faith

The present situation brings an ineluctable hermeneutical task for Christian faith, specifically for theology, its reflective mode, including liberation theology. The paradigms of all the theologies articulated on the basis of modernity are in crisis: their theoretical articulation, their interdisciplinary relationships, and the relevance and significance of their discourse. We need to find new working hypotheses to give an effective response, from faith, to the new questions. One of these is that of certain European and North American theologians, such as Hans Küng, Jürgen Moltmann, David Tracy, and Matthew Fox, who, taking on the emptiness of the subject, propose a non-confessional theology: ecumenical, macro-ecumenical, ecological, and holistic.

In Latin America, particularly in Brazil, two attitudes are emerging in the face of the crisis. On the one hand, there is that of certain groups who, taking advantage of the crisis of modernity, stress the importance of *emotional understanding*, based on the religious experience of the new Pentecostal movements that are in the ascendent worldwide. Here emotionalism and fundamentalism function as factors of security, really a false security. On the other hand, there is the approach of militant groups pursuing social causes directed at the *humanitarian* (human rights, civil organizations, a culture of solidarity, ecology) and *mystical* (personal religious experience, inter-religious dialogue, and rejection of the institutional) aspects. This approach would point to the irreversibility of the process of laicization of Latin American cultures. Also not to be ignored, and also with implications for theology, is the generalized recourse to other, non-Western, models of society: the Hebraic-biblical, indigenous, African, Oriental, and other worlds, which is more than an expression of *light* culture. It expresses the search for new bases for fragmented and disillusioned Western civilization.

As can be seen, in the midst of the perplexity of a modernity in crisis, people are searching for a new *theological aesthetic*, one that can make its epistemic relevance penetrate the age of *hermeneutical and communicational reasoning*, forming a *hermeneutical-contextual-social theology*. This brings with it the inescapable need to reconstruct collective identities, in three areas: the social (communicational reasoning), the epistemological (hermeneutical reasoning), and the ecclesial (theological reasoning).

II. The challenge of the world of insignificance

It was the church in Latin America that introduced poverty as a viewpoint for the hermeneutics of the Christian faith: How can we speak of God in a world of crucified people? How can we view salvation history in relation to a human history marked by injustice? The great legacy of the church on this continent has been to provide a response, from faith, to the critique of religion as alienation. Through its practice and reflection on this, it has sought to pass the central motives for the credibility of the gospel through the filter of historical proof. This has involved emphasizing the option for the poor against poverty as an evangelical criterion. From this viewpoint, we have made a reality of the whole of revelation from within liberation theology. On this point Brazil, with Leonardo and Clodovis Boff, João Batista Libânio, Frei Betto, Jose Comblin, and Hugo Assmann, among others, has made an outstanding contribution.

1. Liberation theology: theology for Latin America?

Nevertheless, although liberation theology came from Latin America, it is not a theology solely for Latin America. All theology is contextualized, and poverty is a reality for all, one that challenges the understanding of Christian faith as a whole. All are challenged by the unity between the plan of creation and the plan of redemption, once sin has become a disorder within creation; by the distinction without separation between evangelization and human advancement, because there is a continuity between work for building a just world and salvation; by salvation as moving from less human to more human situations, since the kingdom of God has an immanent and historical dimension, which means postulating the existence of a single history and the bringing about of salvation within the core of this history, which is at once secular and salvation history, and so on. In other words, concepts such as justice, freedom, human dignity, and the like are not alien to salvation. Faith and love are authentic only when they are effective. It is not enough to have a Christianity of good intentions, correct in doctrine but uncommitted to reality. The whole of faith has to be set in the whole of life, and so it should also shed light on and transform politics, economics, culture, society, and the rest.

2. A challenge: broadening the concept of the poor

There is, however, no doubt that history has changed. In Brazil, since the end of the 1980s, we have insisted that we cannot go on conceiving the phenomenon of poverty purely in economic terms. We are faced with the challenge of investigating the world of insignificance, of examining all its different aspects. In doing so, we have found the theory of dependence, while not a false instrument, inadequate for taking account of the phenomenon in all its many facets. The concept of 'poor' has to be broadened today to include those discriminated against or excluded by reason of their race, language, culture, colour, gender, age, and so on, which makes poverty a situation present everywhere on all continents, including the northern hemisphere.

3. A call to action and reflection

The fact that history has changed and the face of poverty become more complex cannot be made an excuse for not acting or reflecting. In Brazil, we have to be concerned over the shift from militancy to mysticism and the restriction of this to the private sphere, over the exuberance of emotion in religion and the theological vacuum, particularly in some church movements tainted by fundamentalism. The poor are still there, poorer than ever, questioning the credibility of our faith. Theology, or the understanding of faith, being a second step, needs practice, the first step, in order to compose its discourse, since praxis, rather than being just the place where orthodoxy comes to earth, is the prime source for the composition of orthodoxy itself. In the context of modern rationality, truth has to pass through veracity; failing that, the very credibility of the gospel is put at risk.

III. The challenge of pluralism

Pluralism too brings a hermeneutical task to Christian faith. In the cultural sphere, the church in Africa in particular has shown us the challenge of an inculturated evangelization, of a pluri-cultural church, and consequently of a theological pluralism. In the religious sphere, the church in Asia above all, further back in history, brought the theological value of difference to the fore, drawing the consequences for the understanding of Catholic dogma in dialogue with non-Christian religions.

In Brazil, the challenge posed by cultural and religious pluralism to the hermeneutics of Christian faith is very strongly present. A proof of this is the reactions aroused by *Dominus Iesus*. Pluralism calls theology to an epistemological and methodological reformulation.

1. Semantic reformulation

For a long time the word 'theology', as used in Christian circles, was seen as the exclusive property of Christianity. Speaking of theology meant referring to the regulated and formalized discourse on faith within the bosom of the Christian churches, specifically in the West and in the First World. The term 'theology' was virtually restricted to a church-centredness stemming from a mono-religious stance, itself a hangover from mediaeval theocracy as taken over by Euro-centrism, the fruit of a monocultural Christianity.

The emancipation of pluri-cultural and pluri-religious acceptance imploded traditional theological semantics, forcing theologians to widen the concept of theology, so as to enable it to take the new emergent realities under its wings. The results have been mixed, more successful in some areas than in others. One of the completely unsatisfactory results, which can also be seen here, is a theological semantics that shifts from a mono-religious and mono-cultural theology to the other extreme, to a trans-cultural and trans-religious theology. It jumps from a 'Christian theology' to a 'world theology', to a meta-narrative made up of interaction of the various religious traditions existing on the planet. As Jacques Dupuis has pertinently observed, such theological pluralism comes up against two obstacles: one is the singularity of the different religious experiences; the other is the singularity of the many cultural matrices that underlie these experiences. A more satisfactory course would be to start from the presupposition that theology embraces many confessions and many cultures.

2. *Syntactical reformulation of theology*

(i) Embracing many confessions. The existence of 'religious faiths', distinguished from one another by their actual content, means that the diversity of contents of the various expressions of faith inevitably gives rise to a diversity of confessional theologies. As a regulated and formalized discourse of faith, theology cannot not be confessional, since the actual content of each religious experience is seen in adherence to faith by individuals and communities, which, in the final analysis, are the object of theology. The confessional character of theology, however, is not exhausted within its own confessional group. On the contrary, the confessional group itself will be better explained to the extent that it is open to the totality of the religious experience of humankind. What belongs to a confession, if it lacks a genuinely universal horizon, leads to confessionalism, which is the road to fundamentalism, incapable of recognizing, or of recognizing itself in, other religious denominations and of enriching itself with other confessional theologies.

(ii) Embracing many cultures. In the cultural sphere, a trans-cultural world-wide confessional meta-narrative comes up against the plurality of the religious experiences of the different religious confessions, even within a single confessional group. An intentionally trans-cultural confessional theology will still be a mono-cultural theology, the universalization of a particular special entity, to the extent that the working out of its meta-narrative will not escape the contingencies of a particular culture.

Therefore, theologies are not only confessional but also pluri-cultural, for two reasons: first, that any confessional entity exists in a pluri-cultural context; second, that all religious experience within a particular confessional entity also comes about in its own cultural context, which is different from the context of the religious experience of other communities within the same confessional group. Theology is always a human product, inevitably bound to the 'paradigm of a period' (Thomas Kuhn). However much it may want to, it can never do without the sum total of convictions, values, modes of thought and action shared by a particular community. This in no way impoverishes interpretation of revelation: on the contrary, it frees it from becoming an ideology, as it also frees theology from turning itself into fundamentalist discourse.

So, while in the religious sphere there cannot be one trans-confessional theology but must be several, in the cultural sphere, within the confines of a single religious confession, there can only be different theologies, in the sense of diverse expressions of a single faith lived in the heart of cultural diversity. And given that, from the cultural point of view, these intra-confessional interpretations, including the Christian one, are developed from diverse cultural matrices, we are left with the inevitability that theology, besides being pluri-confessional, will also be pluri-cultural.

What is different about a pluri-religious and pluri-cultural type of theology as compared to a trans-confessional and trans-cultural theology is that the former will seek to prioritize reality over abstraction, existence over essence, ultimately the living experience of persons in their communities, in specific circumstances, over concepts and generalities deriving from a religious and cultural myopia.

Pentecostal Flames in Contemporary Brazil

BRENDA MARIBEL CARRANZA DÁVILA

Starting from a plural and de-institutionalized religious context, I want here, more descriptively than analytically, to (a) set out the changes brought about by the phenomenon of Pentecostalization, both Protestant and Catholic, in the religious field in Brazil over the past thirty years, focussing attention on two emblematic examples: the Universal Church of the Kingdom of God and the Movement for Catholic Charismatic Renewal, in its popularized version led by Fr Marcelo Rossi; (b) sound a warning on the mechanisms of *spiritual warfare* that have developed between charismatics and neo-Pentecostalists in their battle for followers, a scenario that has become a religious market place; and (c) show the impact Pentecostalism is having on the resolution of routine and existential problems in public life and the media.

I. Pentecostalization in Brazil

A double process can be seen at work in the religious field in Brazil: the deepening de-institutionalization of certain sectors of the middle classes, leading individuals to a growing privatization of religious experience, and the appearance of a plurality of Pentecostal religious expressions and institutions, breaking the monopoly held by the Catholic Church (Sanchis 1997).

This Pentecostalization has re-configured the religious profile of our society in the last thirty years. According to the census by the Brazilian Institute of Statistical Geography (IBGE 1991) the population was divided into: Catholic faithful, including traditionalists, progressives, nominal, and non-practising (75%); Protestants, divided among historical churches (12.5%); and Pentecostal and neo-Pentecostal churches (7%);[1] Spiritist followers of Kardec (3%), persons who declared themselves members of Afro-Brazilian religions such as Umbanda and Candomblé (1.5%);[2] the remainder, made up of minority religions such as Jewish, Muslim or Oriental, plus those with no religion (Prandi & Pierucci 1996).

The Pentecostal presence, both Protestant and Catholic, has brought about changes in the speech, practices and piety of many Brazilians.[3] Both versions share belief in the daily presence of the Holy Spirit and the efficacy of its miraculous gifts and healing of ills of body and soul. Pentecostal religious practices are notable for the assiduous particpation of their faithful in worship and intra-institutional activities (Mariz 1998).

Its manifestations include clapping, speaking in strange tongues (glossalalia) and uncontrolled shouts of praise and bodily movements. The verbal treatment of the devil is aggressive, dismissive of mediumistic religious expressions, especially Afro-Brazilian ones, although in practice its rites of liberation and exorcism incorporate symbolic elements taken from these, taking over and re-signifying what it rejects, attacks, and demonizes (Birman 1996). Besides this, both Pentecostals and charismatics take part in many and creative mass activities (meetings in football stadia, gymnastic displays) as well as carrying out works of charity.

Another point they share in common is the use of music to attract young people and to animate religious 'spectaculars'. Here the salient figure is the young charismatic priest Marcelo Rossi, with a background in gymnastic schools feeding into Catholic liturgical performance, dancing and singing to a 'Jesus' aerobics' rhythm and bringing thousands of Catholics together for so-called 'show-Masses'. Furthermore, the singer-priest is creating a genre within the Catholic Church. There are now more than a dozen priests, not counting the seminarians who aspire to the same status, who sing, dance, and appear on television shows to give the same sort of performance (Carranza 2001b). This phenomenon suggests new paths for the training of the Brazilian clergy, concerned as it is for its numerical survival, prestige, and social advancement, replacing dogmatics with studies of guitar and aerobics (Benedetti 1999).

II. Emblems of Brazilian Pentecostalism

At the centre of the Pentecostal scenario stands the Universal Church of the Kingdom of God (IURD), founded in Rio de Janeiro in 1977 by Edir Macedo, whose personal religious trajectory included belonging to Afro-Brazilian religions (Umbanda). The IURD is one of the fasting-growing neo-Pentecostal churches[4] in the country, spreading into other countries in Latin America, Africa, and Europe.[5]

The IURD has mounted a grandiose apparatus for itself, making its places of worship in cinemas, factories, or other buildings designed to hold thousands of people. Its preaching is focussed on self-help and on the divine exchanges between the faithful and God in the challenge to achieve prosperity. The morality preached by its pastors is on the 'light' side compared to the asceticism of other Pentecostal churches. Characterized by a strongly hierarchical and centralized power, it has evolved a vertical structure that leaves little space for participation by its millions of followers (Mariano 1999).

Not far from this description is the Movement for Catholic Charismatic Renewal (RCC), accused of being a Catholic version of evangelical belief on account of its Pentecostal forms of expression. In the last decade, the RCC has evolved strategies for affirming its own identity (wearing rosary beads; poster campaigns – 'I'm happy because I'm Catholic'; adoration of the Blessed Sacrament; distribution of papal images and speeches; insistence on personal confession), while reiterating its faithfulness and belonging to the Catholic Church. At the same time, it has become the chief protagonist of Catholic teaching and orthodoxy, above all in the realm of sexual morality.

Although the process of acceptance of the RCC in Brazil has been the outcome of a controversial and ambiguous journey lasting twenty years,[6] relations between its lay leadership and the Catholic hierarchy seem to have wavered among three attitudes on the part of the clergy: first, *suspicion* of its use of emotion, manipulation of gifts, and lay autonomy; second, *assimilation*, since charismatics are a potential source of a not negligible pastoral workforce for the institution, with their ten million followers organized in prayer groups and allied communities and found in most of the dioceses; third, *domestication*, shown in the recognition that the RCC can be a containing wall against the flight of faithful to Pentecostalism and might prove a ready source of vocations to the religious life or the priesthood (Carranza 2000). This institutional force penetrates the private sphere through its practices and teaching, forming a new ethos through the need for conversion it preaches to its followers. It exhorts its followers to an exclusive adherence to the institution, offering them symbolic goods and services in exchange.

III. Magical solutions to historical problems

Both members of the IURD and leaders of the RCC are extremely creative in the replies they give to the faithful seeking remedies for their afflictions. At IURD services, RCC cenacles, and Fr Marcelo's masses, one can often see thousands of believers offering up prayers for healing and liberation, in the hope of being cured of incurable diseases or psychic disorders. One can also access Fr Marcelo's website (www.padremarcelo@.terra.com.br.) to take part in the blessing of remedies.

These expressions relocate human suffering, mixing the allopathic therapeutic system with elements with a symbolic meaning (prayer, blessing, water . . .). The same happens in the face of the scourge of structural unemployment. One can often see the faithful holding up work permits or photographs of relatives who are alcoholics or drug-users, for them to be blessed by Fr Marcelo or the IURD pastors (Steil 2001; Mariz 2000). The same strategies to give new meaning to health are used in the divine axis of salvation. There is nothing more traditional in popular culture than divine intervention in suffering, nothing more advanced in the information society than the internet, nothing more convenient for a free-market economic system, which preaches a minimal state, than replacing the health care infrastructure with religion. These are the elements that make Pentecostalism an extremely vigorous religious phenomenon.

IV. Exorcism in the realm of power

The public sphere of national life is the target of Pentecostal leaders who preach ethics in politics, given the spiral of administrative corruption. In the past decade we have witnessed an ascending scale of electoral success for the IURD, which now has twenty-six federal deputies in the legislative assembly, as well as some state deputies and town councillors.[7] For its part, the RCC in the national Congress is led by a federal deputy who speaks for the block of Catholic deputies. More revealing than their numbers are the strategies both groups have evolved to gain access to power.

To assess its electoral prospects, the IURD carries out an opinion poll among its members, then launches its own candidate, who is presented at all events organized by the church (at services, mass meetings, on TV, in the press and on the radio), emphatically promoting the fact that this is the official candidate; it makes use of charitable activities to make the candidates circulate. In this process, the prerogative of choosing a candidate belongs to the local leaders, who follow their calculations and interests, counting on the fidelity of members of the institution, on the personal charisma of the leadership, and on its capacity for transforming pastors into candidates (Oro 2001).

In the same way, the RCC is not indifferent to its electoral potential and, discreetly but not without tensions with local churches, uses its organizational capability to motivate, promote, support and elect candidates from within the ranks of its leadership. The RCC carries out its offensive in the

National Congress, where charismatic leaders make moralizing speeches defending the teaching of religion in public schools. It also promotes actions against state campaigns to prevent the spread of AIDS and against free distribution of condoms. It militates against legal proposals to legalize homosexual unions and to carry out abortions in public hospitals for victims of rape.[8] The political activity of the RCC is worth pointing out, since this demystifies a certain consensus that saw the CEBs, linked to liberation theology, carrying out the political struggle, while the RCC occupied itself with spiritual care in the Catholic Church.

The IURD uses the religious sensitivity of its directors to work on the senses of its followers/electors: that is, it transforms the act of voting into a *quasi religious* act, to the extent that it becomes a sort of exorcism of the devil present in politics and responsible for corruption. Once he has vacated this space, the *men who fear God* can occupy it. Besides the sacralization of politics this implies, the fact that other religious bodies are now adopting this way of doing politics gives rise to concern (Fonseca 1998). Just as the individual sphere is the target for Pentecostal expansion and the public sphere is the *locus* of God, so in the battle for faithful the media will become the setting for *spiritual warfare* with its all-out anti-syncretic discourse.

V. Marketing, the soul of evangelization

In October 1995, under the heading 'Fall of the Saint', the Brazilian media recorded the attack made by an IURD pastor on an image of Our Lady 'Aparecida' (patron of Brazil). On a television programme, broadcast live, the pastor tossed the image into the air, denying it was a sacred object and condemning Catholic idolatry in worshipping images. The incident and its consequences placed the country on a holy war footing, aggravating the dispute between charismatics and neo-Pentecostals, with television as the battlefield.

In Latin America, tele-evangelism has become known as the 'electronic churches' (Assmann 1986). In Brazil in the 1990s their expansion was consolidated, with a considerable increase in the output of religious programmes. Some churches created their own networks; others hired time, increasing competition through electronic catechesis. In the neo–Pentecostal sphere, TV Record, whose purchase by the IURD is the subject of a legal process, has relegated most of its religious programmes, proselytizing in tone and preaching personal conversion, to the mornings.

These programmes rely mainly on the use of words, in which, with tears, sighs, close-ups, and melodramatic videos, people give their personal witness. The format is always the same: the faithful tell their life story, emphasizing how they found a reason for living through 'paths of sorrow' and telling how, when they joined the church, they overcame their existential and economic crisis – the latter common to the majority of Brazilians, but which in audio-visual language is stripped of any connection with the social situation.

Thanks to the experience built up by the RCC through its independent stations, and to the support of the Brazilian bishops, it has been possible to create a national TV channel, *RedeVida* (Life Channel), as the channel for Christian families. It provides news of church events, transmits televised masses and rosaries, and makes TV an extension of parish life (Carranza 2001a).

In this scene, Fr Marcelo Rossi, sponsored by a large multinational and blessed by Pope John Paul II, rules the digital market as the Catholic Church's new field of evangelization. Here the singer-priest displays his extreme dynamism in generating a huge trade in religious goods and services under the name of Byzantine Sanctuary.[9] Besides this, Fr Marcelo is the 'logo sign' of the most powerful internet service provider, Terra, which commits him to events such as opening the largest IT Fair, singing and dancing on the Terra stand. With chatrooms, WAPs, and the *iBest 2000* (a prize for the most visited site in the 'personality of the year' category), the religious pop star guarantees faithful-consumers. While this priest is the exponent of modern catholicity, he has become a consumer good and a publicity tool for a sector of the Catholic Church that seems to have bet on religious marketing as the salvation of evangelization. Its followers swing between electronic pulpits and digital churches, turning thmselves from spectating faithful to surfing faithful, all seeking answers to their material and emotional afflictions in the Brazilian religious market place.

Conclusion

In the end, the process of Pentecostalization reinforces the re-traditionalization of the Brazilian religious scene. Through its expressions of competitive institutional plurality and its daily activities, tied to 'only correct' interpretations of the world, the Pentecostals are taking a fundamentalist direction. Expressions of Brazilian Pentecostalization affect mainly the poorer sections of the population, with their folk religion proving to be the new marketing niche for large and small entrepreneurs.

At the roots of the Pentecostal ascendancy one can see its antennae for connecting with the popular world of images, rooted in sufferings and demons. Furthermore, the ideological and cultural affinities (cronyism and authoritarianism) present in national politics are reinforced by the individual, subjective nature of Pentecostalism's tenets, increasingly far removed from any possibility of social transformation.

The field of the media is fertile ground for debates, for gaining, converting, and keeping followers, showing itself ever more creative in its combination of religious and economic interests. So Brazilian Pentecostalization advances with one foot in pre-modernity, in its preaching and practice, and the other in post-modernity, through its use of technological means, re-creating the modern Brazilian tradition.

Notes

1. As is well known, the historical emergence of Protestant Pentecostalism dates from the beginning of the twentieth century, in the USA, with records of its arrival in Brazil going back to the first decade (Freston 1994). Catholic Pentecostalism, known as Charismatic Renewal, arose in the 1960s, also in the USA, with its cradle in university circles. The movement expanded rapidly, reaching Brazil in 1969 through two Jesuit priests (Benedetti 2000; Carranza 2000).

2. The cult of possession in Afro-Brazilian religions consists in a communication delivered by the *orixás* (divinities), through divinatory means (intervention of elements or mediumistic revelation). The Pentecostal churches carry out exorcisms on people who have already taken part in these initiation cults, regarding them as needing to be freed from the supernatural source of witchcraft (Birman 1997).

3. This diocesan priest, born in 1968, is described in the media as athletic, charming, agile, charismatic, strong, happy, relaxed, empresario . . . but above all as singer-priest turned pop star. In October 2001 the men's magazine *Penthouse* named the singer-priest the 'marketing missionary', questioning the destination of the money earned by Fr Marcelo, reckoning this in millions of dollars just from his recent CDs. With the support of his diocesan bishop, Fernando Figueiredo of Santo Amaro/SP, Fr Marcelo sets out to attract Catholics bored with the church, preaches doctrinal and catechetical truths in the form of slogans, and appears in TV programmes for various audiences together with singers and presenters famous nationally and internationally.

4. The Pentecostal expansion in Brazil came in three great waves: the first (1910–50) began in the north of the country with the coming of the Assembly of God Church and the Christian Congregation of Brazil; the second (1950–70)

coincided with the move to the cities and formation of mass societies, with the Quadrangular churches and Brazil for Christ and Love; the final wave began in the 1970s, in the period of dictatorship and modernization of communications, with the IURD, House of Blessing, and International Church of Grace as its main exponents (Chesnut 1997; Freston 1994).

5. The IURD has a presence in Portugal, France, Angola, Mozambique and the USA, principally among Hispanics. On 31 October 2001 it was given the concession for a TV channel in the United States, to be distributed by Dish Network, an EchoStar company, targetting Brazilians living in the States.

6. Pressured by the growing visibility of the RCC in the media, by the clergy and public opinion in general, the Brazilian bishops found themselves forced to produce the document 'Pastoral Orientations on Catholic Charismatic Renewal'. In it they legitimize the existence of the RCC, approve of its activities within the church, and warn of some 'exaggerations' in its demonizng preaching and practice of exorcism.

7. Research shows that in the 2000 elections in the state of Rio Grande do Sul the IURD launched 63 candidates (pastors and workers), of whom 19, some 30% of the total, were elected, an unimaginable proportion for a political party. In the capital, Porto Alegre, the two official candidates showed the IURD's political potential, collecting 19,000 votes, more than all the other religious denominations together (Oro 2001).

8. Charismatics put strong pressure on the Commission for the Constitution, Justice and Citizenship over its review of Law 209/91, which obliges hospitals bound to the Single Health System (SUS) to carry out abortions provided for in the 1940 penal code.

9. The Byzantine Sanctuary, besides being a place for liturgical celebrations attended by thousands of people, is a large business managed by the priest's family, selling veils, rosaries (blessed and exorcised), caps, and CDs, all carrying the Byzantine Sanctuary trademark. In order to counteract piracy it has adopted the strategy of organizing a competition for those who buy the original CDs, with the prize of a journey to Rome, including an audience with the pope.

Bibliography

Hugo Assmann (1986), *Igrejas Eletrônicas e seu impacto na América Latina*, Petrópolis: Vozes.

Luiz Roberto Benedetti (2000), *Templo, Praça e Coração: articulação do campo religioso católico*, São Paulo: Humanitas – FFLCH/USP – FAPESP.

——(1999), 'O Novo clero: arcaico ou moderno?' in *Revista Eclesiástica Brasileira* 233 (Mar.), pp.188–226.

Patrícia Birman (1997), 'Males sem remédio e esperanças de cura' in *Tempo e Presença* 9 (Nov.), Rio de Janeiro.

—— (1996), 'Cultos de possessão e pentecostalismo no Brasil: passagens' in *Religião & Sociedade* 17, 1 (Aug.), Rio de Janeiro.

Brenda Carranza (2000), *Renovação Carismática: origens, mudanças e tendências*, Aparecida, SP: Santuário.

—— (2001a), 'Da igreja eletrônica para a igreja digital' in *Anais do IV Encontro de Antropologia do Mercosul. Forum: Olhares novos e distantes do campo religioso* (Nov.), Curitiba, Paraná, Brasil.

—— (2001b), 'Paroquialização da televisão: respostas educativas?' in *Anais do Encontro de Comunicação e Educação contemporânea* (Nov.), ed. Faculdade de Educação, da Universidade de São Paulo (USP) – Faculdade de Comunicação, da Universidade Anhembi-Morumbi São Paulo.

Chesnut, R. Andrew (1997), *Born Again in Brazil: The Pentecostal Boom and the Pathogens of Poverty*, New Brunswick, NJ: Rutgers University Press.

David Dixon & Sérigio Pereira (1997), 'O novo protestantismo latino-americano: considerando o que já sabemos e testando o que estamos aprendendo' in *Religião e Sociedade* 18, 1 (Aug.), Rio de Janeiro.

Paul Freston (1994), 'A Igreja Universal do Reino de Deus' in *Nem Anjos nem Demônios: interpretações sociológicas do pentecostalismo*, Petrópolis: Vozes.

Alexandre Brasil Fonseca (1998), 'A maior bancada evangélica' in *Tempo e Presença* 302 (Nov.-Dec.), São Paulo: CEDI.

Ricardo Mariano (1999), *Neopentecostais, sociologia do novo pentecostalismo no Brasil*, São Paulo: Loyola.

Cecilia Loreto Mariz (1998), 'Changements récents dans le champ religieux brésilien' in *Social Compass* 45, 3 (Sept.).

—— (2000), 'Uma análise sociológica das religiões no Brasil: tradições e mudanças' in *Cadernos Adenauer* 9, São Paulo.

Novo Nascimento (1998), in *Relatório de pesquisa: Os Evangélicos em casa, na igreja e na política*, Rio de Janeiro: MAUAD.

Ari Pedro Oro (2001), 'Religião e Política nas Eleições de 2000 em Porto Alegre' in *Debates do Núcleo de Estudos da Religião (NER)* 2, 3 (Sept.), Universidade Federal de Rio Grande do Sul, Porto Alegre.

Reginaldo Prandi (1997), *Um sopro do espírito*. São Paulo: EDUSP-FAPESP.

—— & Flávio Pierucci (1996), *Realidade Social das Religiões no Brasil*, São Paulo: Hucitec.

Pierre Sanchis (1997), 'O Campo religioso contemporâneo no Brasil' in Oro & Steil (eds), *Globalização e Religião*, Petrópolis: Vozes.

Carlos Alberto Steil (2001), 'Pluralismo, Modernidade e Tradição:Transformações do Campo Religioso' in *Ciencias Sociales y Religión / Ciências Sociais e religião*, 3, 3 (Oct.), Porto Alegre.

Tendências do Catolicismo Atual (2000). In *Relatório de Pesquisa*, 2. Centro de Estátistica Religiosa e Investigações Sociais (CERIS) & Instituto Nacional de Pastoral (INP). Rio de Janeiro.

Women in the Brazilian Church

MARIA CLARA LUCCHETTI BINGEMER

Practically a whole century has passed since the start of the phenomenon of women's emergence in all sectors of social, political, and cultural life in the Western world. And the fact of this emergence has generally been recognized as one of the most important and significant factors contributing to the changed profile of that world today. The female half of the human race, emerging from the shadow of invisibility after so many centuries, merits attention and interest from specialists in many different areas. To see the truth of this, one only has to look at the great quantity of research, writing, and events organized on the subject, relating it to the most diverse areas of learning and knowledge.[1]

The religious sphere has not been able to stay away from this common and global effort. Since the most ancient times, and in all religions, women's presence and experience have been decisive in – and for understanding – the inner structures of communities, their rites and different forms of expression. Many of the tribal religions of primitive societies and poytheistic religions in general display a strong presence of the feminine element, either in relation to the part women play in the ritual and institutional organization of the religious group or in relation to the concept of the sacred and the divine that underlies the basic experience and doctrinal *corpus* of these religions. This can still be seen today in African religions or, closer to us, the Andean religion. In some religions, women's experience and insertion into the community take place in terms of a journey of personal integration on the way to a proper and 'visible' situation on the level of life in public and within the social framework as a whole.

The Judaeo-Christian religious tradition, however, does not wholly fit into this framework. Valuing women's role above all as wives and mothers (Judaism and Christianity) or in a state of virginity consecrated to God (Christianity), it has thereby restricted women for centuries almost solely to the domestic and private realm (home or convent). This is reinforced by the fact that in Judaeo-Christianity the image of women is nearly always associated with sin and, therefore, with temptation, seduction, and danger, thanks to the biblical tradition of Genesis, which gives woman the leading role in the fall of humanity and so-called original sin.[2] So women, harbingers of menace, generating fear, have been increasingly confined to private, domestic, or conventual spaces, where they can more easily be controlled and silenced.[3]

The winds of female emancipation in the West did not blow, therefore, from the churches in the first place. On the contrary, it was as part of the whole secularization process and within very specific and secular struggles (over the vote, wages, working hours, sexuality, rights over their bodies) that women made their 'escape' from the private domestic space to which they had been confined and out into the public arena, taking part in social organizations, in politics, in economic life and cultural affairs.[4]

The coming of women's emergence to the Christian world does not seem to date back more than four decades. After the great event of Vatican II, women's voices began to make themselves increasingly heard, claiming their right to occupy places in the church and effectively putting this into practice: through taking on community leadership at various levels, through questioning the impossibility of access to the priestly ministry, reserved exclusively to men,[5] by the production of theoretical reflection on religious experience and the doctrinal contents of the faith from their own women's viewpoint.[6]

I. Women in the church south of the Equator

To try and portray the situation of women in the Brazilian church we need, then, to trace the religious and ecclesial course of women in terms of their process of coming to understand their commitment and their sense of belonging to the religious institution as such. Furthermore, we need to see how this process applies in terms of the services and ministries women are currently providing to the church in Brazil. I indicated at the start that I see this process as linked – to a greater or lesser extent – with women's developing consciousness with regard to their role in history and in the structures of society and with their effective assumption of this role within various political bodies.

To achieve this objective – on the one hand, that is, to recover the religious and ecclesial journey made by women from the popular communities in terms of their process of understanding their commitment and belonging to the religious institution as such and, on the other hand, to see how this process is linked – we can build on the main anthropological framework that permeates the whole question of women's presence in the private and public spheres and which is expressed in terms of (1) the question of gender relations, and (2) the question of the socio-political-cultural background of the women we are concerned with.[7]

The first aspect to draw our attention as a seam of theological reflection is the demystification that the most recent feminist literature produced in Brazil and eleswhere in Latin America has brought to bear on the struggle for equality as the central objective of women's causes and aspirations. While this concerns women of the middle classes, who have sufficient to live on and are educated, it concerns the women of the people even more: living on the margins not only of this movement but of the whole process of the modernization of society, they are only now beginning to be affected by the struggle, and they are beginning to draw conclusions different from those of their intellectual or professional companions. Women – and Christian women to a particular degree – at this juncture of history are not trying or wanting to reproduce the way men – masters of public space – carry on their struggle. Their way is different, their field of action is different, their manner of interpreting the world is different. The women of the people, confined more than any to that private sphere from which they have never been allowed to emerge, have far more reason than others not to be moulded by masculine society as such, and so have the opportunity to devise something new on their journey towards liberation and participation.

Approaching the question in more theological terms, we see that this movement and this journey are a real re-creation for women, so deep is the discovery of themselves they are making in the course of this process. Theology, which has only recently applied itself to the question of women, is now trying to examine the matter on the basis of biblical texts, the gospels, and church practice.

II. When women begin to believe in the 'other' woman

As soon as women – and mainly women of the people – join together with other women, who reflect back the multiplicity and plurality of their features, a new situation emerges and it becomes possible for them to see themselves in a new and different way.[8] Furthermore, they are then enabled to aspire to spaces and actions beyond those they have reached and achieved before now. Comparison with the Bible helps in this, giving it a foundation. The Old Testament – which is also a basic text for Christians – is already a source of texts that, if not explicitly in favour of women, are nonetheless susceptible of 'recovery' in a new hermeneutics: Genesis 3, for example, is an account recently re-examined by women, who have shed significant new light on it.[9] In the same way, research into and study of the New Testament have shown, for example, how Jesus behaved in relation to the actual women who were close to him, how he re-created them out of his own nature, brought them to recognize him as Messiah and Son of God, and so led them to a process of 'exogeny' or 'exodus' from the place imposed on them for centuries, sending them out into public places to bcome agents in the building up of the kingdom of God.[10]

Specifically, in Brazil and elsewhere in Latin America, women and above all the women of the people who are organized and linked in Bible-study groups, mothers' clubs, and base church communities are being able to feel this 'new thing' that comes from a new manner of being together, sharing their problems and hopes, and from new contact with and possibilty of interpreting the Bible and the words of the gospel. This is definitely making them into new agents in the church, which is not necessarily expressed in terms of enlarging institutional space for themselves within the church as such. Nor does it bring in its train, as one of its primary claims, access to ministries until now denied to women, such as the priesthood and other ordained ministries. It does, though, involve a human and religious experience that opens new routes and new doors.

Observation of women, especially those of the people, seems to show that this experience is a passageway to another 'new thing' – the building of a public space and exercise of citizenship in a new way, on the basis of 'difference' restated as a valuable and important element in the whole process, including a redefinition of the very concepts of 'public' and 'private'.

III. Women taking on charisms and ministries in the church

The course of the recent history of Christian religions and churches in Latin America, and most notably in Brazil, has shown an original and consistent dynamism on this point. In Brazil specifically, since the 1980s, the face of the church has been marked by various major changes brought about by women.

1.The great majority of those who take part in religious activities are women. Among these, some 80% are from 'popular' social backgrounds, meaning that they live at poverty level, subject to all sorts of oppression. For many of these women, their journey through Christian religious and ecclesial experience has proved to be a steady and genuine access route to emancipation and recovery of their human dignity, offering a real and original possibility of access and passage to greater social consciousness and taking their place in the public sphere, in terms of taking part in trade uinions, in neighbourhood associations, in popular movements, and in political parties. If these women from the poorer reaches of society are still thoroughly oppressed in the family, the workplace, and civil society, their effective participation in the religious and ecclesial sphere has shown them that there are other possibilities.

The religious experience and activity of Brazilian women of the people and the fact that they have, in huge numbers and as a majority, taken on various ministries in the church often initially provide them with the only space where they are allowed to be present and active beyond the domestic limits of household and family care. The fact that the Catholic Church in Brazil has, in many of its dioceses, adopted the ecclesial model of CEBs (base church communities) alongside and beyond the traditional parish model, in which services were still excessively concentrated in the hands of the priest, has allowed many women to realize their capabilities and potential for co-ordination, leadership, and organization.

2. Since the 1980s, women have been providing new services in the church, another witness to the 'new thing' that is coming about through women and from them. Women are no longer just carrying out their traditional functions of catechesis, looking after churches and presbyteries, and the like, but also increasingly fronting communities, being committed pastoral agents, taking responsibility for whole groups of people, organizing their needs and seeking access to the official services of the church for them in the most effective way possible.

3. The presence of women in the field of spirituality has also grown to a notable extent. Countless women in Brazil today, lay or religious, devote themselves to preaching retreats, providing spiritual counselling on an individual basis, and producing material to help constructive preparation of prayer and liturgy on all their different levels. These spiritual teachers have made an outstanding impression, helping many men and women through their own feminine appreciation of God and experience of the Spirit characterized by their feminine manner of being.

4. Then there are the women theologians. After going through a whole – and by no means easy – process of discovery of themselves and of their role within the theological community, women are studying in theological

institutes in ever greater numbers, obtaining academic qualifications, and proving expert at the ministry of theological teaching and research. The theological production stemming from their hearts and minds is reaching an ever greater degree of maturity, meaning that it is no longer focussed just or mainly on the subject of women but on all aspects of theology, seen and studied from their perspective as women. Lecturers and writers, researchers and intellectuals of solid depth, women theologians enable one to say that theology in Brazil would today be unthinkable without their contribution. If they were lacking, a major part of theological reflection, a basic approach to outstanding problems, a unique 'breath' that only they can give to the ancient yet ever new themes of the Christian mystery would also be lacking.

5. Among the subjects that have been dear to the women who have become more intensely active in the church in Brazil since the 1980s, and particularly to women theologians, two (besides the actual subject of women themselves and all the theological and biblical themes seen from women's viewpoint) stand out as especially significant. They are polemical and – ecclesially speaking – delicate, and the initial approaches made to them by Christian women in the 1980s were timid and cautious. Nevertheless, their importance and centrality meant that they were increasingly discussed, and the early 1990s saw them emerge as great challenges to theology done by women.

The first of these is the area of ethics and morals that deals with reproductive rights and sexuality. There is a vast field to be explored here, given new force and reinvigorated elements, particularly for Catholic women theologians, by Pope John Paul II's encyclical *Evangelium Vitae*. Since the 1980s it has become clear to women that the challenge of thinking through their bodiliness, sexuality, and fecundity in the light of Christian revelation and in dialogue with the Magisterium of the church is a mission they cannot avoid. They have taken up this mision and continue to do so with courage and hope.

The other subject is more linked to the sphere of ecclesiology. This is the question of ministries. All women involved in services within the church feel in their flesh how urgent the need is for reflection and practice that respond to the wishes of the people of God on this matter. Women began to respond to this situation effectively in the 1980s by taking on various ministries in the communities. The 1990s saw further progress along this road, following fruitful though not always easy paths opening on to new vistas of possible and promising developments in the direction of increasingly enabling

Christian women to find an intra-ecclesial route to their transition from the domestic to the public arena.

It is on the basis of these central and vital points that I see the role of women in the Brazilian church evolving in the new millennium just begun, glimpsing the new horizons that are opening up with it. And in this new thing that is already begun, there is, finally, something characteristic of women's contribution to the future of the church that cannot be ignored. These women, despite their often hard and even crushing daily lives, are full of hope and confidence. Life and the world do not strike them as threatening and destructive but, on the contrary, as full of possibilities for living and for building something that is greater and better than what they have been and are experiencing up till now.

Notes

1. Some of the more recent research from Brazil and Latin America includes: R. M. Muraro, *Sexualidade da mulher brasileira. Corpo e classe social no Brasil*, Petrópolis 1983; F. Tabak, *Autoritarismo e participação política da mulher*, Rio de Janeiro 1983; A. Sojo, *Mujer y política. Ensayo sobre el feminismo y el sujeto popular*, San José 1985; C. Lora (ed.), *Mujer: víctima de opresión, portadora de liberación*, Lima 1985; F. Tabak, *Mulher e democracia no Brasil*, Rio de Janeiro 1987; *O impacto da urbanização sobre as mulheres de baixa renda*, Rio de Janeiro 1987; G. Sen and C. Grow, *Development, Crises and Alternative visions. Third World Women's Perspectives*, New York 1987; J. Astelarra, *Feminismo. Autoritarismo. Democracia*, Rio de Janeiro 1988; S. Pimentel et al., *A mulher como objeto de estudo*, Rio de Janeiro 1988; D. Patal, *Brazilian Women Speak. Contemporary Life Stories*, New Brunswick and London 1988; M. Régia et al., *Como trabalhar com mulheres*, Petrópolis 1988; J. Astelarra, *Feminismo. Teoria e prática*, Rio de Janeiro ²1989; *A mulher no terceiro milênio*, Rosa dos Tempos, Rio de Janeiro, 1992.

2. On this point, see the analysis of the creation narratives made by M. C. Correa Pinto, *Mulher e política*, São Paulo 1992. See also the opportune and pertinent reflexion Pope John Paul II has made in his *Mulieris Dignitatem*. The pope restates original sin as the sin of the whole human race and not only or principally that of woman. Other works among the vast bibliography on this subject include: P. Saint Yves, *As virgens mães e os nascimentos miraculosos*, Rio de Janeiro 1960; P. Evdokimov, *La femme et le salut du monde*, Paris 1978; L. Boff, *O rosto materno de Deus*, Petrópolis 1979; R. Radford Ruether, *Sexism and God-Talk*, Boston and London 1983; E. Rae and B. Marie-Daly, *Created in her Image. Models of the Feminine Divine*, New York 1990; M. C. Bingemer, *O*

segredo feminino do mistério, Petrópolis 1991; I. Gebara, *As incômodas filhas de Eva*, São Paulo 1991; P. Aquino, *Nuestro clamor por la vida*, San José 1992.

3. On this see what J. Delumeau says in *História do medo no Ocidente*, São Paulo 1990, esp. pp.310–49, 'Os agentes de Satã: III. A mulher' (Portuguese trs of *La peur en Occident*, Paris 1988; English trs *Sin and Fear: The Emergence of Western Guilt Culture*, New York 1990). See also J. M. Aubert, *La femme. Anti-féminisme et christianisme*, Paris 1975, and other works.

4. Cf. C. Meillassoux, *Mulheres, celeiros e capitais*, Porto 1976.

5. It is important to note that this claim has already become a reality in other mainstream churches, where the ordination of many women priests and even of some women bishops has become an everyday event. In the Roman Catholic Church, however, it has not happened yet.

6. As witness the plentiful and expert theological and exegetical publications by women, especially in First World countries. In Brazil and elswhere in Latin America such publications, though still at an early stage, have increased considerably over the past seven years.

7. Note that I am using 'political' here not in its strictly party political sense but in a broader sense, meaning intervention in the situation and structures of society with the intent to change them.

8. See T. Cavalcanti, 'Produzindo teologia no feminino plural. A propósito do III Encontro Nacional de Teologia na perspectiva da mulher' in *Perspectiva Teológica* 52 (1988), pp.359–70.

9. See E. Pagels, *Adam, Eve, and the Serpent*, New York 1989; also M. C. Correia Pinto, *Mulher e política*, São Paulo 1992.

10. Theology, particularly that done by women, has produced numerous works on this aspect. See especially T. Cavalcanti, 'Jesus, a pecadora pública e o fariseu' in *Estudos Bíblicos* 24 (1989), pp.30–40; I. Gebara, 'Cristologia Fundamental' in *Revista Eclesiástica Brasileira* 48 (1988), pp.259–72; M. C. Lucchetti Bingemer, 'Jesucristo y la salvación de la mujer', in *Aportes para una teologia desde la mujer*, Madrid 1988, pp.80–93; *O Segredo Feminino do Mistério*, Petrópolis 1991; A. M. Tepedino, 'Jesus e a recuperação do ser humano mulher' in *Revista Eclesiástica Brasileira* 48 (1988), pp.375–9; *As discípulas de Jesus*, Petrópolis 1990.

Afro-Brazilians and the Church: Open Wounds, Scars, and Hopes

AFONSO MARIA LIGORIO SOARES

I. The drama of Brazilian slavery and African identity

The press in Brazil has recently published the results of a survey comparing the annual average income of Brazilians, taken from UN statistics – which placed Brazil in 69th position in the world – with a number of other researches carried out on a national level, by households, by the Brazilian Institute for Statistical Research. Using the methodology of the UN Development Program, Professor Marcelo Paixão of Rio de Janeiro concluded that if white Brazilians were considered separately, their average income would put them in 46th position worldwide (in the high development bracket), while the Afro-Brazilians would fall to 101st position.[1] This social debt of Brazilian society to those of African descent is an integral part of the history of the whole country. Brazil was the major importer in the black slave trade: 38.1% of the Africans who reached America were destined for the then Portuguese colony.

This huge contingent of slave and non-citizen population gave the whole history of the colony and the subsequent empire its dominant tone. In the first census of Brazil, made in 1572, out of the 52,000 inhabitants, 28,000 (53.8%) were African slaves, and 14,000 were listed as indigenous (meaning those already 'integrated'). The remaining 10,000 inhabitants included children of indigenous mothers and Portuguese fathers as well as those of pure Portuguese descent. The 1817 census still showed black slaves as the majority of the population. This is without counting freed slaves, those in runaway slave settlements, and those of mixed race. In short, we are a nation that has, throughout most of its history, held a majority of its population in captivity, subjugated by the slavery regime – a population of non-Brazilians.

Even the abolition of slavery, towards the end of the nineteenth century, was full of contradictions. It was advanced by two groups: the emancipationists, who were merely concerned to replace the labour force with immigrants, to enable Brazil to modernize; and the abolitionists, who defended abolition as just bringing compensation for the slaves (through agrarian reform) and their integration into society. The first group was victorious, meaning that Brazil entered the twentieth century with an enormous number of ex-slaves and their descendants who quite simply had no idea what the right to have a family and property implied.

Nevertheless, although the social scar produced by Brazilian slavery should in no way be underestimated, one has to recognize black creativity in rebuilding – in its own fashion – the greater African family, as, for example, in the case of *candomblé*, of the runaway slave villages (whose remaining communities are still fighting for legal recognition of their lands and their culture),[2] of the brotherhoods, of the samba schools, of the contemporary black movement. Appreciation of this black epic is a basic element in fashioning the identity of Afro-Brazilians, an identity whose political affirmation is, in the words of K. Munanga, the only way of escape from the ideological traps concealed under the camouflage of the concept of 'half-blood'.[3]

II. Experience of the sacred: the Afro-Brazilian contribution

In view of the picture painted above, how can we speak of the history of evangelization in Latin America without mentioning the conquest and cultural transplant carried out by the dominant religion? This is not a question of judging and condemning the possible good intentions of the church leaders of that time. The church, in effect, found itself faced with an undertaking comparable only to the Christianization of the barbarian races it had embarked on in the early Middle Ages. But there is one important distinction to be made: before, the conquerors were the barbarians, and the evangelizers had to make at least some effort to enter into their *modus vivendi*. On the soil of Latin America, on the other hand, only a few timid and isolated initiatives aimed at teaching were risked. The Africans and the survivors from pre-Colombian times were forced to take the (qualitative?) Christian leap in a short space of time. And, because of this, they were happy to take on the exterior trappings of Christianity, effectively hiding – deliberately, at least in the early days – their age-old archetypes.

So, even while the European religious system overlaid African religion during the colonial period, it did not succeed in taking its place. Black slaves read the Catholic pantheon, overflowing with saints and Virgin Marys, in the light of the relationships between intercessory *orishas* and Olorum. The (cultural) reading of the saints as lending their patronage to various human activities helped to make them like *orishas*, including those who governed particular sectors of nature – Xangô, lighting and thunder; Oiá-Iansã, winds and storms; Oxum, fresh water – or protected different occupations – such as Ogum, who protects all sorts of metalworkers. With a deft touch of imagination, the slaves were able to find a way of importing the Catholic saints into their own pantheon. For example, to provide an analogy between Oxalá and Jesus Christ, no more was needed than the external resemblance between the aged Oxalá with his walking-stick and Jesus the Good Shepherd with his crook. Through procedures like this, the blacks reinterpreted many Catholic feasts. Exu is celebrated on St Bartholomew's day; Xangô on St John's; Ogum shares the commemoration of St George; Omolu that of St Sebastian; the Ibejis (*orishas* of childhood) share the feast of SS Cosmas and Damian; Oxalá shines in New Year festivities (in Bahia, on the feast of Our Lord of Good Death); and Iansã stands in for St Barbara.[4]

Furthermore, by putting aside the Catholic ideology of 'suffer in this life to be happy in the next', African religion actually purifies devotion to the saints. Besides this, members of *candomblé* themselves take part in the life of the Catholic Church – to the point where, if someone is not a Catholic, he or she cannot take part in a 'yard' ceremony. So, as can be seen, despite all their adversities, the African peoples are able to make a creative synthesis out of their tragic experience in the 'Atlantic inferno'.

III. African religions in Brazil: from persecution to dialogue

There is an urgent need for Brazilian Catholics to turn to an attitude of dialogue with the religions of African origin, most particularly with their brothers and sisters who belong to two religions (Catholicism and *candomblé*, for example). The first obstacle to this remains, however, the rooted prejudice that still predominates. Since the beginning of the last century, and with the more or less tacit approval of the Catholic hierarchy, *candomblé* houses and, later, *umbanda* tents were systematically raided by the police. Political-religious diversity was thereby recorded as belonging in the dossiers of frequent crime. Some writers went so far as to claim that religions of African origin were a source of criminality. Early psychiatry in the country soon placed *umbanda* on the list of causes of mental illness – along with syphilis, alcoholism, and contagious diseases. The trance phenomenon was wrongly interpreted as possession and associated with hysterical symptoms and madness.

Once embarked on this tide of attacks, the Catholic Church preferred, instead of dialogue, to proceed against 'the adversary'. This was how Cardinal Motta lamented the situation, a few years before the last Ecumenical Council of the Vatican:

> Besides the fetishism of our indigenes and of those peoples originating in Asia and Europe, our people have received this unfortunate native heritage also from Africa, by means of the former black slaves . . . It is sad to note that the march of our spiritual and cultural progress has been from church to parlour, and not from parlour to church. *Macumba* is one of the greatest threats to faith, to morality, to our rights to education, to hygiene, and to security, It is the alarming indication of our religious and scientific ignorance, and of the lack of protection afforded to us by the police.[5]

In a spectacular about-turn, Friar Boaventura Kloppenburg, former leader of orthodox campaigns against Spiritists and Umbandists, had this to say some years after the council:

> Africans, when they become Christians, do not renounce their identity but take on the old values of their tradition in spirit and in truth. We, however, because we were Europeans, Westerners, members of the Latin Church, of the Roman Rite; we who sang to the sound of the organ and prayed on our knees in sacred silence; we who were incapable of imagining a sacred dance to the beat of drums; we wanted Africans, just because they were living alongside us, to stop being African, to adopt a European and Western mentality, to integrate into the Latin Church, to pray in the words of the Roman Rite, to sing to the solemn sound and rhythm of the organ, to abandon their native dances, their rhythms, their animated prayers. It was the total, proud ethnocentrism of Europeans and of the Church that came from Europe. But blacks, once they became free, no longer accepted our rites, no longer enjoyed our harmonies, no longer spoke in our concepts; they went back to their yards, to their drums, to the rhythms of their origins, and to the myths of their language. From the depths of their beings, where living and unquiet, the religious archetypes of previous generations were still beating, the old religious tradition of Black Africa burst forth. And *Umbanda* was born in Brazil.[6]

Despite testimonies such as this one, however, we still bear ancient wounds in the relationship between the Catholic authorities and the black community. We are beginning to think about these wounds now that Afro-Brazilians are speaking out both inside and outside the Christian churches, in a process of reclaiming their ancestral traditions and with them their dignity.

IV. Challenges and hopes: black pastoral agents

The year 1983 was paradigmatic in the recent history of dialogue between Christians of African and of European descent. From 17 to 23 July that year, Salvador da Bahia was host to the *Second World Conference of Orisha Tradition and Culture*. At the end of the conference, in a printed manifesto, five of the most respected *ialorishas* published the polemical decision to break with Afro-Catholic syncretism, on the grounds that 'our religion [is] not a sect, a primitive animist practice; consequently, we reject syncretism as a fruit of our religion, since it was created by the slavery to which our ancestors were subjected.'[7]

Two months after the Bahia manifesto, a Christian (mainly Catholic) event brought new subjects into this discussion, ratifying for the future a more positive vision of the black traditions within the Catholic Church itself. After a long period of incubation in small groups spread all over the country, the *First National Meeting of* (what were thenceforth known as) *Black Pastoral Agents* was held in São Paulo in September 1983. Second and third meetings were held in May and September of the following year. The inaugural meeting led to the formation of the *Central Quilombo* as the general secretariat of Brazilian black pastoral agents.[8]

These black pastoral agents from the outset claimed a degree of autonomy from the Catholic hierarchy, as also from political parties and other ramifications of the Black Movement.[9] From the start they insisted on a posture of dialogue among the Christian churches and among the different religions. With this, they intended to increase their ability to move into and mobilize the black communities.

The future of relations between the church and the black community in Brazil has, since then, been linked to developments in the actual practice of the black pastoral agents. The churches, and particularly the Catholic Church, are becoming blacker. This partnership has already produced considerable progress, with results that have re-kindled our hopes. One might quote the pioneering 1988 Brotherhood Campaign, which courageously tackled the forbidden topic of Brazilian racism. It also dealt with increasing the numbers of ecumenical groups of black pastoral agents to work beyond Brazil, with developments in centres for black seminarians and religious; the by then traditional Meetings of Black Priests and Bishops; the formation of the Atabaque Group to study black culture and theology;[10] which has since inspired the founding of similar groups in other Latin American countries; many initiatives by NGOs aimed at achieving full citizenship for the 46% of the population of African descent; and so on.

The flagship policy of the Catholic majority of the black pastoral agents over the past two decades has been the recovery of black traditions and the reaffirmation of their cultural identity. And this inevitably raises the question of how to deal with the prevailing syncretism, or double religious belonging, of members of the Afro-Brazilian community. How far can committed Catholics allow themselves to go on the quest for their authentic African roots? Is it possible to revere *orishas* and profess the Catholic faith at one and the same time? The difficulty of dealing with this question emerged clearly from two international consultations that brough black militants from various contries together.[11] Antonio A. da Silva has placed, among others, the subject of 'ecumenism and macro-ecumenism (integral ecumenism) from the African perspective' on the agenda for the next meetings.[12]

In brief, what is at stake here is how the black pastoral agents and other sectors of the church deal with Afro-Catholic syncretism. Even black militants have so far been puzzled by the question. In the end, what are we dealing with? Mixture and confusion? 'Popular ecumenism' or 'macro-ecumenism'? Will spirituality be our point of contact between the riches of *candomblé* and the Christian tradition? Or is it enough to isolate the phenomenon of syncretism as a cultural expression that does not force one to renounce the Catholic faith? Could the purely folkloric use of *candomblé* symbols in Catholic worship, even if in a slanted fashion, result in some committeed Catholics discovering the tradition of their people in the black religions?

Such hesitations lead on to other questions: What might the true function of the churches be in these situations of (apparent) religious miscegenation? What services should Christians provide in such contexts? Is the good of the people served by converting them (en masse) to a more 'orthodox' Christianity? In short, is the salvation-liberation of the people of God synonymous with 'mature' personal adherence to the community we call church?

The eventual replies to these questions will either be found in the outcome of the numerous experiments being made by the black Brazilian community, in dialogue with the different sectors of the church, or they will simply not be replies for anyone.

Notes

1. Cf. *Folha de São Paulo*, 6 January 2002.
2. Today, the communities that seek to benefit from being classified as 'remnants of *quilombos*' in order to secure their right to the lands on which they live, do not necessarily have to be made up of descendants of runaway slaves. According to the definition by the Brazilian Association of Anthropology, a *quilombo* is 'any rural black community that contains descendants of slaves living by a subsistence culture and where the cultural manifestations have a strong link with the past.' (Cf. 'Relatório final do grupo de trabalho criado pelo decreto n° 40723 de 21/03/96' in ITESP, *Quilombos em São Paulo*, 47).
3. K. Munanga, *Rediscutindo a mestiçagem no Brasil*: identidade nacional *versus* identidade negra.
4. R. Bastide, *As religiões africanas*, vol. 2, pp.376–80. Saint-*orisha* features and equivalencies are not, in any case, the same all over Brazil. Xangô is St Jerome in Bahia, the Archangel Michael in Rio de Janeiro, and St John in Alalgoas. Exu is the devil in Bahia (perhaps of account of his 'trickster' character), St Antony in Rio de Janeiro, and St Peter (here understood as doorkeeper of heaven and messenger of the gods) in Rio Grande do Sul.
5. Cardinal Motta, 'Combate ao Espiritismo' in *Boletim Eclesiástico*, Archdiocese of São Paulo (July 1953), p.302.
6. Cf. B. Kloppenburg, 'Ensaio de uma nova posição pastoral perante a umbanda', p.410.
7. Cf. J. G. Consorte, 'Em torno de um manifesto de ialorixás baianas contra o sincretismo' in C. Caroso and J. Bacelar (eds), *Faces da tradição afro-brasileira*, pp.71–91 (here pp.88–9).
8. The same year also saw the birth of a Black Seminarians' Group, initially bringing together students from the archdiocese of São Paulo and from the Institute of Theology of São Paulo (ITESP).
9. Despite the sympathy of the majority of militants of the period for the nascent Workers' Party·
10. Atabaque was founded in 1980. It is an ecumenical NGO that brings together theologians and other students of the Afro-Brazilian cultures. Its purpose is to back up the thinking and practice of black pastoral agents, and it also promotes exchanges with international groups and bodies concerned with the subject.
11. I refer to the *Iª Consulta sobre Cultura Negra e Teologia na América Latina*, Duque de Caxias-RJ 1985, and to the second, *Consulta Ecumênica de Teologia e Culturas Afro-Americana e Caribenha*, organized and managed by the Atabaque Group, São Paulo 1994.
12. A. A. da Silva, 'Elementos e pressupostos da reflexão teológica a partir das comunidades negras – Brasil' in Atabaque-ASETT, *Teologia afro-americana*, pp.49–72 (here p.65).

Church and Politics in Brazil Today

FRANCISCO WHITAKER FERREIRA

The great problems facing Brazil today in the political sphere are ethical in character: social inequality and the behaviour of the politicians in power. The first is structural and the second personal, and they feed off one another; the economic structure that creates inequality stems from a political culture of individualism, which encourages the quest for personal power and wealth; structural changes are of no interest to the privileged – including those in political power.

There is no doubt that the social inequality of Brazil today is a major scandal. It is made up of concentration of wealth, which is among the greatest in the world, and of the disparity in earnings between those with the highest income and those with the lowest.

The 'included third' of the population – as the Brazilian consumer market is generally known – is a number equivalent to the population of the larger European countries. It is therefore sufficient to make a powerful economy function, even through crises. A significant percentage of these consumers have high purchasing power, owing to the concentration of wealth, which makes Brazil an attractive target for corporations from the wealthy nations seeing wider markets. The pressure to open our commercial borders is ample evidence of this.

The scraps that fall from the tables of the rich suffice to fulfil the many needs of rather more than another third of the population – those struggling non-stop to gain a foothold on the lower slopes of the 'included third'. This still leaves almost another third stuck in the bands of the 'excluded'. And more than half of these live in destitution and hunger. Ever more concentrated in the cities, where there is insufficient work for them, this section of the population – numerically significant – can also no longer provide their basic food needs by growing their own crops: in the last forty years the rush to the cities has left less than 20% of the population in the countryside over the country as a whole and less than 10% in some regions.

Within this framework, the whole of the country's productive and commercial system – and even investments in government 'social' infrastructure – functions to the benefit of the 'included third'. Advertising is designed to address only the wants and needs of this third, or creates superfluous needs for it in a climate of runaway consumerism; municipal authorities, for their part, prioritize programmes designed to supply the comforts required by the privileged sectors of their population.

This inability to 'include' more people in the consumer market is not a recent phenomenon. It was even introduced into the legal framework of the country in the nineteenth century, with the Lands Law of 1850. This law, by deciding that ownership of the abundant lands the country then disposed of could pass on only through inheritance or purchase, sought to deny land ownership both to black slaves, then being freed in a process completed four decades later, and – principally – to immigrant workers from Europe, who were beginning to be required to take the place of the slave labour force.

Combined with the complete lack of any limitation on the size of properties (at the same period the United States passed a law defining a maximum extent), the Lands Law divided Brazilians into two classes: the great landowners on one side (a minority from whom many of the 'included third' of today are descended) and those condemned to remain simple sellers of their labour on the other. It was only considerably later that foreign immigrants – though virtually never descendants of black slaves – began to benefit from the Brazilian government's new 'colonization' programmes, especially in the south of the country, or acquired sufficient wealth to 'buy' lands. But it was only with the coming of industrialization and the arrival of fresh waves of overseas immigrants in the early twentieth century that the 'included' began to amount to a third of the population, the process being associated with urban economic activity.

A further factor is that during the whole of its history Brazil has never managed to escape from the capitalist system, which is by nature excluding. Critique of this system and attempts to change the developmental model being followed were both blocked by the military dictatorship in the second half of the twentieth century, at a time when social pressures for change were growing. When governments were once again elected, little progress was possible. On the contrary, those elected to succeed the military opted frankly for a capitalism subject to interests outside the country, openly embracing models of political economics imposed by multinational capitalism, as part of the current process of free-market globalization – the very process that is making the framework of social inequality and wealth concentration worse across the whole world. A 'minimum state' policy, of privatization of essential services, of making currency stability a major objective, is replacing the rights of 'citizens' by the rights of 'consumers', in which what counts is purchasing power. In this way, new forms of 'exclusion' are beginning to affect – and to exasperate – social sectors that had formerly thought themselves safe.

The striking thing is that the social inequality and concentration of wealth that make up this dispiriting picture form an environment regarded as 'natural' and accepted by rich and poor alike. It does not provoke indignation, as though it had nothing to do with ethics. The rich are ostentatious with their wealth, with their mansions and imported luxury cars. The poor are content with fulfilling their role on the production ladder or in the chain of commerce. In the latter thousands – if not millions – of 'itinerant vendors' are even subjected to regulations in the larger towns and cities. All the destitute can do is 'importune' the other two thirds where the police allow them to – leading those who own cars in the big cities, for example, to fit them with air-conditioning so that they can keep the windows firmly shut.

In these early years of the twenty-first century a sense of insecurity and violence is spreading. Organized criminals and drug traffickers are operating ever more openly, leading to zones in the poorer quarters of the big cities where they are in control, where the state cannot manage to make its presence felt. The rich are beginning to find it necessary to have their cars armour plated – an economic activity expanding rapidly in Brazil. And kidnaps, feared even by the middle classes, in which small or large sums are demanded for the release of hostages, are multiplying to the extent that they are becoming commonplace: the media now refer to 'kidnaps in progress' and 'completed kidnaps'. Indignation is shown only when the 'bandits' are cruel or when someone emerges to protest that the 'human rights' of potential prisoners are being violated. In a police and prison regime in constant crisis – revolts against the extremely precarious conditions of prisoners are an almost daily occurrence – torture and even massacre of prisoners can take place without any great reaction from society. The increase in violence by criminals is even making many people want to bring back the death penalty.

The way social injustice and even crime have become commonplace is in keeping with the second ethical problem in Brazil today – that of personal behaviour. The individualistic and consumerist ethos currently prevailing, which leaves little room for indignation to express itself, encourages the acquisitiveness of the privileged classes. Among these, most politicians regard their activities purely as a form of personal self-enrichment.

Structural changes recede from the framework of their concerns. Privilege depends on maintaining the present economic status quo.

The gate is thereby opened wide to corruption, backed up by the impunity that was most evident in the way protesters were repressed during the military dictatorship. Eroding the credibility of 'politicians', corruption also damages the general behaviour of society, which sees it as 'an example that comes from the top'. There are those who say it has by now become endemic. Ethics in politics and in the conduct of public affairs has become something exceptional, despite the efforts of many and the initiatives undertaken by the social services, which despite everything are beginning to show evidence of change.

In this overall picture, what challenges face the church in Brazil in the sphere of politics? The greatest challenge is obviously the complete incompatibility between what is happening and the gospel message of peace, justice, brotherhood, and social equality. What has the church done or failed to do to prevent the current situation coming about, and what should it do to close the enormous gap in the spreading of its message?

Perhaps a more decisive contribution from it in this direction was not to be expected. Its activities directed at bringing about change in the political climate are relatively recent, taken in the context of Brazil's history: as actions of the institution and of the church, as opposed to those of isolated pastors, they began only fifty years ago. It was only in the mid-twentieth century that its bishops began to act as a body in this area. Their 'brotherhood campaigns' began to deal with social and political themes a mere thirty years ago, after a series further aimed at taking the measure of Vatican II, which re-situated the universal church in regard to 'the social question'. The year 2000 campaign, besides being the first to be organized by an ecumenical council (CONIC, the National Council of Christian Churches), of which the Bishops' Conference was part, returned to the path previously trodden by making Human Dignity and Peace its theme.

During the last fifty years, the church took part (before the military coup of 1964) in struggles for 'grassroots reforms' aimed at securing the social changes then beginning to be required, and during the military regime then installed it played an important part in the struggle to re-democratize the country – despite the support given to the coup by some among its ranks. It denounced torture and the 'National Security' law and protected many who opposed the military regime. During this period the base church communities also began to flourish, and they became increasingly involved in the struggles of local communities for more worthy conditions of life.

With the end of the military regime, the church took part in social initiatives designed to secure the people's involvement in drafting the new Brazilian constitution and allied itself to proposals such as Citizens' Action against Hunger and Destitution, which originated in secular society with the participation of many lay Christians and even some bishops. In their Assemblies and other decision-making bodies, as well as through the many organizations it established in the realm of social pastoral activity, the church has taken an increasingly firm stance with regard to government policies and has been pressing for specific actions, such as agrarian reform. To a greater or lesser degree, it has criticized the development model adopted by the country's leaders – as over the issue of internal and external debt – and so has often been regarded as the opposition.

Concerned with the processes by which political leaders are chosen, it intervened directly in 1998 in electoral legislation: it led groups from civil society in a 'people's legal initiative' against the electoral corruption that was making use of the people's destitution to keep politicians in power. Once the proposed law had been adopted, the church strove to see it effectively applied in the 2000 election and is now preparing for the next. Another legislative endeavour of this sort is in process, to limit the size of rural landholdings – 150 years overdue.

The Bishops' Conference has recently associated itself more visibly with new efforts being made by society to work out 'another world', such as the World Social Forum, where one of its bodies forms part of the oganizational structure. It is also associating itself with various initiatives in the mass communications media, crucial for forming people's attitudes.

If the church has still not succeeded, in the purely electoral sphere, in getting a majority of political leaders who are truly interested in building a just society elected, its efforts are also still far from overcoming, in society as a whole, the general acceptance of inequality and destitution, of corruption, of the lack of ethics in political behaviour, of the subjection of public policies to interests outside the country, of the substitution of citizens' rights by purchasing power, and so on. The church has still not found a way to make the prophetic nature of what ought to be its witness lead to effective implementation of justice.

Would it make any difference if 'Christians' were more widely engaged in politics, either with elective mandates or not but certainly without the illusion of a need for 'church' parties? If this proved to be the way forward, the greatest task for the Catholic Church in Brazil today in the political field would be in persuading the greatest possible number of 'lay people', prepared to demonstrate the radical requirements of Christian life in their personal behaviour and their actions to transform society, effectively to become 'protagonists' of church action in politics. Unlike the bishops and the clergy, lay people experience the daily difficulties of ordinary citizens, and only they can – and should – take part in the political struggle. How then can they be encouraged – in large numbers – truly to carry out this role as Christians, in the diversity of each one's personal journey and in the unity of the common purpose? And how can they be given power and a voice as church in a society marked by hundreds of years in which the church is heard as such only when the speaker is one of its bishops or priests?

It is not easy for 'lay people' to detach themselves from the prevailing atmosphere of the country and take on, as individuals and as church, the radical demands of the Christian mission for transformation. But perhaps what would be required of the bishops and clergy is still more difficult: to accept that 'lay people' taking part in the world's struggles should also be seen as fully church, so that they can carry out their role integrally, sharing responsibility and communion with the other members of the church. Starting from this, they could then make society accept them as true 'protagonists' of church action.

Open Letter to the Soul of Brazil

PEDRO CASALDÁLIGA

When my Claretian Congregation held its general chapter in 1967, seeking to carry out its duty and will to adapt the Congregation's life and rules to Vatican II, I had the chance to 'take a leap' overseas, to 'go on the missions', as we said in those days, and as I had dreamed of doing since I was a child. Two choices were offered me: the *altiplano* of Bolivia or Brazilian Amazonia. I was open to both. Furthermore, I have to admit that Bolivia held a certain revolutionary appeal, since at that time Che Guevara had just died, in an odour of popular appeal. It was at this stage that the superior general of the Institute, the German Peter Schweiger, advised me to opt for you, my Brazil. 'Pedro,' he said to me, 'Brazil, as a society and as a church, is a land with great challenges and a great future.'

So on 26 January 1968, that year of revolutionary youth, of the arbitrary Institutional Act (A15) that hardened the military dictatorship in Brazil, and of the liberating General Conference of Latin American Bishops in Medellín, I came to you, Brazil, to the warmth of your sun and of your people. We have, then, known each other for a long time, and I can talk to you with the freedom of a friend, as a citizen by now, at least by adoption, and even as a son by upbringing.

I know you well enough to talk to you of our common concerns and hopes. I know you are 'worth the effort' – the effort and the joy – because you are not 'small-minded'. You, Brazil, have a clear call to give a lead: not, of course, in the sense of being a leading power, but of leading in service in solidarity, of setting a coherent example, of providing brotherly encouragement, in our America most specifically but also to a certain extent in relationship with other countries of the so-called Third World, especially with certain African peoples (from whom you also derive and to whom you should return in solidarity). To do so, your first task is clearly to become more Latin American yourself. You often feel yourself to be somehow set apart, like a sort of autonomous continent. Never forget that you are America, my Brazil – Latin America, Amerindia, Afro-America, Our America!

You are wonderfully plural; you cannot ignore this fact of your plural make-up. You contain a large number of the world's cultures. Even out of need, but above all out of a conscious, free, creative choice, you should be welcoming, ecumenical, 'macro-ecumenical'. There can be no room in you for the single-centred smallness of one race or one culture. Few countries in the world have so much possibility or need to be and to feel themselves multi-ethnic, multi-cultural – as indeed the Federal Constitution declares you to be, at least in theory.

You must, above all and once and for all, take on your indigenous and African nature. You have already seen, during your history as 'Brazil', the sacrifice of more than five million indigenous inhabitants. After five hundred years of the ill-named 'discovery' and the beginnings of an ambiguous evangelization, you yourself feel the need for 'another five hundred', to begin a new history, different from the last five hundred. This means taking up the Indigenous Cause effectively, demarcating and guaranteeing their lands, legal and effective respect for their cultures, their autonomy, their inter-integration. Because it is not a matter of integrating the indigenous peoples by disintegrating them but of the various cultures of your people mutually enriching one another. Too much Indian blood has already been spilt; official indigenist policy has already told too many lies. Evidently, all this also calls for a true indigenist re-education of the whole Brazilian people.

Africa is the mother of most of your people. Brazil, you are the second most populous Afro nation in the world, second only to Nigeria. You are, beautifully, a black soul, with all the potentials of negritude when it is taken on with pride, without complexes, overturning prejudices, making space for itself in all spheres of social life – including that of the churches. You are routinely praised for not being segregationist: this is not always justified. You still have, Brazil, an official and popular widespread *apartheid* in access to goods and opportunities. I reckon that, in the face of and opposed to your huge foreign debt, you have an even larger indigenist and Afro debt, as society and as church.

Your so-called 'greatness' comes largely from being the child of migration. You, Brazil, are undoubtedly among the three of four countries in the world that have had the most varied migration. You should face up to this heritage, opening yourself generously to immigrants and granting them legal, peaceful, and opportunity-filled residence, especially when these immigrants are seeking refuge from wars or from natural disasters. You should also accept parental responsibility for your many sons and daughters migrating internally and externally. There is a lot of Brazil 'moving out' or just 'on the move' in the vast homeland of the country or in the world beyond your borders. And you must take notice of this migration and find out what its structural causes are. Generally speaking, all migration, one way or another, is the outcome of a forced and painful decision.

This land of yours, 'gigantic by its very nature', as your national anthem declares, has huge resources of land and water – two riches at risk and subject to injustice. Brazil, you are unfortunately the champion when it comes to concentrating land ownership into a few hands, just as you are nearly the champion at concentrating wealth. Absentee landlordism is still the social cancer of the country, and there will be no peace in the land of Brazil while it exists. Agrarian reform, as well as agricultural reform, is a national need, one that the administrative powers are not willing to tackle structurally and that is being addressed with heroic generosity by movements and pastoral initiatives such as the Landless Workers Movement and the Pastoral Land Commission. The land still to be shared out is soaked in blood; it has a sacred price.

Awareness of the land question has recently been joined by awareness of the water question. Brazil is a huge world reservoir of water. The politics and pastoral approaches to both land and water are two major questions and unavoidable responsibilities for a Brazil seeking to be human and Christian.

You are deeply religious, exuberantly religious, and there is space in you for all faiths and all mysteries, which both your cultural pluralism and a sort of native eclecticism embrace. Yet you have not always found a way to welcome this richness of religious and mystical feeling in peace and clarity. At this time of inter-faith dialogue and mutual respect, you have the pioneering mission of relating your official Roman Catholic faith and that of other Christian churches to folk religion, which is often syncretic in practice. Brazil, you can show the world what it is to be a prophetic laboratory of inter-faith dialogue and co-existence.

Your religious expression is joyful by nature: you celebrate life, dance life; you know how to fill liturgy with light, music, and colour; 'From the stem of life, even wounded, a flower is born, springing from pain,' you fearlessly sing. You very well can – and should – be a witness to hope on this continent 'of death and hope' that is Our America and throughout the rest of the world, despairing to a greater or lesser degree.

Like the whole of Latin America, you used to be almost wholly Catholic. You are still the largest Catholic country in the world. (We could humorously and earnestly debate whether you are the most Catholic country in the world . . .) This has sometimes made you intolerant of other Christian churches. Today you are more ecumenical and you possess ecumenical bodies that are unique in the world, witnessing to a growing ecumenicity. This is the right road to take, Christian soul of Brazil!

Your faith, which has often been denounced as 'ignorant', lacking catechesis, without foundation, divorced from life, has shown itself capable of producing the richest gallery of pastoral initiatives, covering all aspects of human life and reaching broad swathes of society. You have pastoral care for everything and for everyone. You are a model, in many ways, for other national churches on the continent and throughout the world. The spirituality of liberation, the theology of liberation, the Bible in the hands of the people, and the various social pastoral approaches constantly show your church to be the most credible of the country's institutions. Go on being celebration-commitment, faith-love, religion-life!

For all that you are and all that you have and all that you do, do not fall into the temptation of making yourself out to be 'the greatest'. (We tend to take pleasure in viewing Brazil as great in everything, the greatest in everything, even in misfortune . . . though not in football at the moment!) I am speaking to you now with the most passionate sincerity, human and Christian soul of Brazil: reaffirm the basic gospel option, opt for the poor, for the little ones, for the excluded. They – men and women – are the favourites of the living God, those to whom the kingdom belongs. (And speaking of women: recognize the fact that you are still too *machista* by far, my 'Brazilian Brazil', in families, in society, in the church, when it fact it is women who provide the support and the vitality in these families, in daily social life, and on the churches' journey.) The *Conclusions* of Santo Domingo, the Fourth General Conference of Latin American Bishops, recognize the cry rising up from the mouths of the poor of Latin America and the present-day causes of this poverty: 'The gaps in society have widened as the market has been deregulated in an indiscriminate way; major portions of labour regulation have been eliminated and workers have been fired; and the social spending that protected working-class families has been cut back. We have to extend the list of suffering faces that we already noted at Puebla [*Conclusions* 31–39: abandoned children, disorientated young people, segregated Indians and Afro-Americans, landless peasants, badly paid, unemployed, and under-employed workers, marginalized and overcrowded in our cities, old people pushed to the margins of society and of progress . . .], all of them disfigured by hunger, terrorized by violence, aged by subhuman living conditions, and anguished over family survival. The

Lord asks us to discover his own face in the suffering faces of our brothers and sisters' (179).

Be self-critical and critical, free and liberating. Enough of empires, of colonialism, of oligarchies, of privileged élites. You know from a long history how much pain and bitterness they have brought you; you are still burdened with the deadly legacy of their élitisms. 'Colonelism', in the political and social meaning given to the term, continues to be a sore on you and on the whole of Latin America. From colonels and *caudillos*, deliver us, O Lord!

Finally, soul of Brazil, so beautiful and so sinful, so knocked about and so generous: for days, months, years, the best heads and hearts of this country have been trying to devise a 'plan for Brazil', a different Brazil, in which there will be space for all the Brazils with their sons and daughters. You have the honour of and the responsibility for making this 'other' Brazil we dream of into a reality. I know so many of our men and women have dreamed of this well before us. They gave up their time and their security, their lives and their deaths, for such a dream. It is up to you to respond to this legacy of blood with dignity. It was just last July that we once again celebrated the great Pilgrimage of the Martyrs of the Latin American Journey, at the sanc-tuary – unique of its kind – dedicated to these men and women, in the little town of Ribeirão Cascalheira, in this diocese of São Félix do Araguaia, in the state of Matto Grosso, on the threshold of Amazonia. You well know that a nation or a church that forgets its martyrs does not deserve to survive. You must stubbornly witness to the witnesses, live on effective memory, take up the dreams and heroism of the past so as to be able to build a new future. 'Lives for Life', 'Lives for the Kingdom', were the mottoes we sang on our pilgrimage, recognizing the meaning, the commitment, and the utopia that so much blood spilt in martyrdom imposes on you and on the whole soul of the Great Country, Our America, continent of death but above all continent of hope.

I invite you to pray with me, every day – so as to refresh our memory and to re-dedicate ourselves to the causes for which they gave their lives – this prayer of the Martyrs of the Latin American Journey:

God of Life and Love, Holy Trinity:
In fellowship with the Martyrs
of the Latin American Journey,
we praise you and thank you
for the strength you sowed in their hearts

to give their life and death
for Life, in Love.

Like Jesus, they were faithful to the end
and gave the greatest proof.
For Him and with Him
they conquered sin, slavery, and death
and live in glory, pasch at the Pasch.

Pour down on us too your Spirit
of unity, of strength, and of joy,
so that we may give our lives
completely to the cause of your kingdom.

Through these many brothers and sisters,
paschal witnesses;
through Mary, mother of faithful witness,
and through the same Jesus Christ,
who was crucified and raised,
the first-born conqueror of death.

Amen, Axé, Awere, Alleluia!

DOCUMENTATION

'. . . and the earth was without form and void': A brief account of a solidarity visit to Palestine

PAULO SUESS

'The governments should not speak of terrorism in order to conceal a basic evil and to justify the threshold of death and hatred. They should see and concede the truth that there is an evil here which must be healed. This evil is the suppression of a people, the theft of its land and its freedom.'

(from the Easter sermon of the Patriarch of Jerusalem, Michael Sabbah, on 31 March 2002)

At the request of the World Social Forum and on behalf of the Indianist Missionary Council (CIMI) and Brazilian Caritas I flew from São Paolo to Tel Aviv on 9 April 2002 with a small solidarity group. There, other groups of the World Forum from Canada, France, Israel, and Palestine joined our group from Brazil. We Brazilians came with quite specific concerns: with other internationalists, Mario Lill, a leading member of the Movement for the Landless, was virtually cut off from the outside world in the general headquarters of Yassir Arafat in the town of Ramallah; today the Brazilian Franciscan Marcos Antônio Koneski is imprisoned in the Church of the Nativity, at the birthplace of Jesus in Bethlehem, with more than 200 others (religious and Palestinians); Sergio Yahni, an Israeli, deputy leader of the Alternative Information Centre (www.alternativenews.org), was condemned to twenty-eight days in military prison on 19 March because, like 435 of his colleagues, he refused to serve in the Israeli army which – as Yahni wrote in a letter to the Minister of Defence – was waging a 'dirty war against the Palestinian Authority'. Sergio had taken part in the World Social Forum meeting at the end of January 2002 in Porto Alegre.

I. Background information

The basic conflict between Israel and Palestine is a dispute about land. Immediately after the foundation of the State of Israel in 1948 there were 300,000 Palestinians; now there are about 800,000 who, under pressure from Israel and contrary to the UN agreement of 1948, had to leave the territory of Israel, which was their ancestral homeland. Between 1990 and 2001 Israel brought a million immigrants from the former Soviet Union to the country and settled them above all in Palestinian areas. The Palestinians who have been driven out are now the inhabitants of the refugee camps of Jenin, Nablus and many other places, which over the years have become cells of resistance against Israel.

After many wars in the region, the treaties of Oslo (1993–95) finally led to mutual recognition between Israel and the Palestine Liberation Organization (PLO). In 1996 Arafat was elected president of the autonomous Palestinian Authority, but because of the Israeli occupation could only administer individual territorial enclaves, while Israel continued its policy of settlement in the future territory of the State of Palestine.

The clash between Arafat and Sharon is a battle between David and Goliath. The Intifada – the Palestinian rebellion of 1987 and 2000 – always began with stones being thrown against Israeli soldiers. The 3.5 million Palestinians live in poverty, crammed into a land of 6,257 square kilometres, in which 200,000 settlers have been placed alongside them. The power of Israel is not based on the size of its territory (20,770 square kilometres), which is inhabited by 6.2 million people, but on its 3,800 tanks, its 2,000 combat planes and its strategic weapons (biological, chemical and nuclear). Many of the Palestinian leaders and those responsible for law and order have been murdered. The only allies of the Palestinians are the international sympathy which goes out to the victims, the solidarity of the Southern axis and some Arab countries, and the will of the survivors to resist. The watchword 'fighting terrorism' and the historical burden of the Holocaust still provide an illegitimate bonus of immunity when it is a question of putting the question of human rights to the heirs of yesterday's victims in today's crisis situation. Reconciliation and moderation succeed more easily among the victims than among their heirs. I am also afraid of the heirs of the Palestinian victims.

II. Scenarios of our visit

On 29 March Israeli troops again attacked the land promised by the United Nations to the Palestinians. That hardly increased the prospect of peace. Peace cannot be compelled by force of arms. Nor can it be enforced by the suicide bombers of Hamas, Al Aqsa or Hezbollah. Sharon is afraid of a peace process in which he would have to make concessions and refuses to talk with his opponent Arafat. Arafat is time and again forced into a corner by fundamentalist groups. Those who suffer shipwreck do not look at the dirty hands which are held out to them.

1. Ramallah

Our group arrived in Jerusalem on 10 April, and a day later, by complicated detours, managed to get to the centre of the town of Ramallah, which is encircled by Israeli troops. Ramallah is like a cemetery, and a couple of foreigners were the only ones going through the streets. A long conversation with the General Director of the Palestine Medical Aid Committee allowed us to investigate the traces of the massacre there. At the checkpoints we were victims of the inhuman treatment of the Palestinians working outside Ramallah. On this 11 April the military removed the exit barrier for three hours. So we were able to talk to people and take part in a protest demonstration by women in the centre of Ramallah – in the middle of barbed wire and tanks. This was the first protest in occupied Ramallah. After ten minutes the soldiers threw tear gas grenades at us, and the subsequent flight then suddenly made us allies of a special kind, more than the words that we had previously exchanged. A Palestinian woman gave me a handkerchief with perfume to lessen the effect of the tear gas. We had contact by mobile phone with Mario Lill of the leadership team of the Brazilian landless movement in Arafat's general headquarters. The Palestinians, too, are today a movement without land. Mario had got into Arafat's seat of government fourteen days earlier, with around twenty other representatives of the solidarity movement, through a hole in the wall which Israeli grenades had torn open in the night, in order to diminish the danger of a massacre there by an international presence. On 22 April, under cover of the visit of the US Secretary of State Colin Powell, Lill left the general headquarters; he was imprisoned by the military for a day, interrogated, and then taken to the airport in handcuffs and fetters and expelled from the country.

On 28 April there was an agreement between the two parties: the military encirclement of the autonomous Palestinian Authority in Ramallah was removed and in return the alleged murderers of the Israeli Minister for Tourism, Rehavam Zeevi, who were there, were put under North American or British jurisdiction. The day that this agreement was arrived at, Israel occupied the city of Hebron, killed eight Palestinians and wounded twenty.

2. Jenin

Jenin is a small town in the north of the West Bank. At the edge of the town there is a camp with around 15,000 Palestinian refugees. We had information that about 500 people had been killed during the Israeli occupation of the refugee camp. On 18 April the UN observer Terje Roed Larsen declared that he was 'shocked' by the reports that he had heard from the survivors. On 19 April the UN Security Council resolved to send an official delegation to Jenin in order to investigate whether war crimes were committed in Jenin.

On Saturday 13 April, our delegation took part in a solidarity march with aroud 5,000 Palestinians, Israelis and internationalists. One of the reasons for this solidarity process was to give protection to around forty trucks of provisions which were needed in Jenin. Our march was finally stopped around fifteen kilometres from Jenin. The Israeli military promised to let the supplies in if the demonstrators withdrew. What else could we do?

Our group from the World Social Forum had been prepared for this, and we then went into the Palestinian regions with a minibus, where we could talk with the survivors of the Jenin massacre. Our first contact took place in a school. Here we met around 200 men. They had been separated from their families, the majority of whom did not know where they had fled to. They told how the Israeli military arrived on 1 April, by air and land, with helicopters and tanks, and spread terror. The hunt for so-called terrorists has made the hunters themselves terrorists. Violence makes all those involved losers. Ajmad told us that fifty-one rockets were fired from the helicopters. One house after another was occupied and razed to the ground with bulldozers. Everyone ran out of their houses with hands raised; some were immediately shot, others taken prisoner, and yet others were able to hide in caves. A group of young men was driven forward in front of the soldiers as a human shield. The UN Human Rights Commission condemned Israel for mass murder on 15 April. We had a long conversation with one mother who had been able to hide in a cave with her children for four days. When they finally left their hiding place out of sheer hunger, they saw the Israeli rifles pointed at them. But there was no shooting. 'It was the children who saved the mother's life,' said the father-in-law.

3. Bethlehem

Our local conversation partners advised us against a visit to Bethlehem. There the Brazilian Franciscan Marcos Antônio Koneski was in the Church of the Nativity at the birthplace of Jesus. I had a letter of solidarity for him from the Provincial of the Order, which unfortunately I was unable to deliver. Since 2 April, 260 people have been with Fr Marcos in the monastery complex. The 60 religious belong to communities of the Greek, Armenian and Latin rite, and the majority of the about 200 Palestinians belong to the government team of the local civil administration (mayor, city council, police), who sought refuge in the church when the Israelis invaded.

The Franciscan community imprisoned there decided on 12 April to leave the place only after both they and the Palestinians had been given guarantees of peace. The group was under the pressure of an attack on the church which was possible at any time, and might involve a blood bath. The sanctuary of Bethlehem, where it is not a question of 'holy' walls but of human life, is one of the last places that the army has not stormed so far. On 15 April Sharon declared: 'We will remain (in Ramallah and Bethlehem) until the "terrorists" give themselves up.' At night the soldiers turn their loudspeakers to full volume. That is part of the psychological war.

The Guardian of the Franciscans in Jerusalem, Fr Giovanni Battistelli, and his deputy, Fr David Jaeger, still have daily contact by mobile phone with their fellow religious who are encircled. Fr David calls above all for the international solidarity of the Jewish communities. The Franciscan, who is himself an Israeli, believes that their pressure on Sharon could have a positive effect on the withdrawal of the military without bloodshed.

III. Resolution of the conflict

The peace proposals of many politicians, states and solidarity groups, including Israelis, like 'Peace Now', more or less agree on the following points.

1. Palestine and Israel recognize and understand themselves as states without a state religion. No one may inherit his heaven through acts of terror or his land with sayings or claims from the Bible.
2. Israel must accept the frontiers laid down by the United Nations in 1967.
3. Jerusalem must become a bi-national capital by law, with part of the city for Israelis and part for Palestinians.

4. The situation of the Palestinian refugees cannot be solved through the 'fight against terror'. The refugees must be given compensation which makes it possible for them to get out of their slum-like refugee camps. Some of the refugees will want to return to their homeland, under Israeli administration. The desire of the Palestinians to return has priority over new settlements of foreigners (e.g. Russians).

5. An international force (UN troops) must be recognized by both sides, which will supervise the observance of the peace agreement.

What will happen next? Mario Lill is again in Brazil, Sergio Yahni is free, the Brazilian Franciscan Marcos Koneski is still imprisoned in the Church of the Nativity and in God's hand. It is only a few kilometres from the Church of the Nativity to the Church of the Holy Sepulchre. These days 'Sister Death' – as St Francis called death – is the daily companion of the Palestinian people. But Israelis, too, are being senselessly sacrificed. On 12 April, five minutes walk from our hotel, a Palestinian woman from Jenin blew herself up at a bus stop. Another six people perished with her. What can be hoped for in this land, which has become 'without form and void' (Gen.1.2), as if there had been no first day of creation? The Old City of Jerusalem seems desolate. Hotels are cheap, and taxi drivers have no work. Anyone who goes to Jerusalem is asked at home, 'Are you crazy?' In the Church of the Holy Sepulchre the prayer times negotiated among the Christian confessions go by without pilgrims. Because there has been so much murder here, there is emptiness around the empty tomb.

In the ruins of Ramallah I saw children playing hide and seek. May their laughter – this side of solidarity, resistance and reason – be interpreted as the promise of a new world? Sometimes hope is only the little 'nevertheless' which lies in all life that resists death.

Sâo Paulo, 29 April 2002

Translated from the German by John Bowden

Contributors

JOSÉ OSCAR BEOZZO was born in Santa Adelia (SP), Brazil, in 1941, and was ordained priest in the diocese of Lins in 1964. He studied philosophy in São Paulo, theology at the Gregorian University in Rome, and sociology and social communication at the Catholic University of Louvain. He is executive secretary of CESEP (Ecumenical Centre for Services to Evangelization and Popular Education), a member of the executive board of CEHILA (Commission for Study of Church History in Latin America) and a lecturer at the theology faculty of São Paulo Universtiy. His publications include *Trabalho, crime e alternativas* (1995); *Igreja no Brasil: de João XXIII a João Paulo II* (1995); and, as editor for the Brazil area, *Historia do Cancilio Vaticano II* (1995).

Address: Rua Oliveira Alves 164, São Paulo (SP) 04210–060, Brazil.
E-mail:jbeozzo@ax.apc.org

LUIZ CARLOS SUSIN was born in Caxias do Sul-RS (Brazil) in 1949 and has been a Capuchin friar since 1968. He holds a degree in philosophy and doctorate in theology from the Gregorianum in Rome and at present lectures in systematic theology at the Pontifical Catholic University of Rio Grande de Sul and at the Franciscan Higher School of Theology and Spirituality in Porto Alegre. He is visiting Professor at the Theological and Pastoral Institute of the Confederation of Latin American bishops in Bogotá and at the Institute of Spirituality at the Pontifical Atheneum in Rome. His publications include *O homem messiânico* (an introduction to the thought of Emmanuel Lévinas, 1983); *Moral emergente* (1989); *Assim na terra como no céu* (1995); and *Jesus, Filho de Deus e filho de Maria* (1997) and articles in the fields of Faith and Culture and Religious Anthropology. He has been President of the Brazilian Society of Theology and Religious Sciences since 1998.

Address: Facultade de Teologia, Av. Ipiranga 6681, 90619-900 Porto Alegre (RS), Brazil.
E-mail: lcsusin@pucrs.br

LUIZ EDUARDO W. WANDERLEY is a university lecturer and a sociologist. He was rector of the Pontifical Catholic University of São Paulo from 1984 to 1988. His publications include *O que é universidade?* and *Educar para Transformar*, besides numerous contributions to collective works and articles in specialized journals.

E-mail: marilew@uol.com

LEILA AMARAL holds a doctorate in social anthropology. She is 'guest lecturer' for the post-graduate course in religious studies and a researcher at the Social Research Centre of the Federal University of Juiz de Fora.

Address: Rua Marechal Deodoro 268, 36013–000 Juiz de Fora-MG.
E-mail: leila.amaral@artnet.com.br

CARDINAL ALOÍSIO LORSCHEIDER was born in Rio Grande do Sul on 8 October 1924 and became a Franciscan at an early age. He was ordained priest on 22 August 1948. After working for some years in convents in Brazil and in Rome he was appointed bishop of Santo Ângelo in Rio Grande do Sul and was consecrated on 20 May 1962. He took part in all sessions of Vatican II and was elected to membership of the Commission that worked on ecumenism. He has been president of the National Conference of Bishops of Brazil (CNBB) and of the Episcopal Council of Latin America (CELAM). In 1973 he was transferred to Fortaleza, in Ceará, where he remained for twenty years as metropolitan archbishop. He was appointed Cardinal by Paul VI. In 1995 he was again transferred, as metropolitan archbishop, to Aparecida, in the State of São Paulo.

Address: Rua Barão do Rio Branco 412, Centro, 12570–000 Aparecida-SP.
E-mail: daloisio@uol.com.br

LUIZ ALBERTO GÓMEZ DE SOUZA was born in Rio Grande do Sul in 1935 and holds a doctorate in sociology from the University of Paris. A national and international director of JUC, he worked for the Brazilian Ministry of Education and the FAO for a number of years. He is a researcher at the John XXIII Centre, lectures at universities in Rio de Janeiro, and reports for the CNBB on social and pastoral affairs. He is currently Executive Director of the Centre for Religious Statistics and Social Investigations (CERIS). He has published articles in Brazilian and international journals and collaborated in various collective works. His books include *O cristão e o mundo* (1965); *Classes populares e Igreja nos caminhos da história* (1982); *JUC: os estudantes católicos e a política* (1985).

Address: Rua das Laranjeiras 525, apto 1002, Laranjeiras, 22240–002 Rio de Janeiro-RJ.
E-mail: luizalberto@ceris.org.br

FAUSTINO TEIXEIRA was born in Juiz de Fora-MG in 1954 and is a lay theologian with degrees in philosophy, science of religion, and theology. He received a doctorate in Dogmatic Theology at the Pontifical Gregorian University in Rome in 1985, with a thesis on the base church communities in Brazil. He returned there in 1997–1998 for a post-doctorate course under the tutorship of Jacques Dupuis. He lectured in the theology department of the Pontifical Catholic Universty of Rio de Janeiro from 1978 to 1982 and from 1986 to 1992. Since 1989 he has been assistant professor of the Theology of Religions on the post-graduate course in Religious Studies at the Federal University of Juiz de Fora and course organizer since 1993. He is also a consultant to the Institute of Religious Studies (ISER/Assessoria) in Rio de Janeiro. His publications include *A gênese das CEBs no Brasil* (1988); *A espiritualidade do seguimento* (1994); *Teologia das religiões: uma visão panorâmica* (1995); *Os encontros intereclesiais de CEBs no Brasil* (1996).

E-mail: teixeira@ichl.ufjf.br

TOMÁS BALDUINO was born in Posse-GO in 1923 and is a Dominican. He was a missionary and bishop to the Indians and settlers in the diocese of Conceição do Araguaia, Pará. He is a co-founder and was second president of CIMI and is a co-founder and current president of the Pastoral Land Commission. He is also bishop emeritus of Goiás-GO.

Address: Rua 242 n.100, Setor Coimbra, 74535–060 Goiás-GO.
E-mail: cptnac@cultura.com.br

JOÃO BATISTA LIBÂNIO was born in 1932 and is professor of theology at the Jesuit Centre for Higher Studies in Belo Horizonte-MG. He is founder-president of the Brazilian Society for Theology and Sciences of Religion (SOTER) and a *rapporteur* for the Inter-Church Meetings of the base church communities. His most recent works are *Eu creio – nós cremos:*

Tratado da Fé (2000); *Introducão á vida intelectual* (2001); *As lógicas da cidade* (2001); *Crer num mundo de muitas crenças e pouca libertação* (2001).

Address: Caixa Postal 5047, 31611-970 Belo Horizonte-MG.
E-mail: isiprof.bhz@zaz.com.br

CARLOS PALACIO was born in Pedreña in Cantabria, Spain, in 1942. He is a member of the Society of Jesus and has lived in Brazil since 1960. He studied theology at Louvain and gained a doctorate in theology at the Gregorian in Rome in 1975. He teaches theology at the Jesuit Brazilian Centre of Higher Studies. His published works include *Jesucristo: historia e interpretación* (1978); *Vida Religiosa inserida nos meios populares* (1980); *Cristianismo e história* (1982); *Reinterpretar a Vida Religiosa* (1991); *Deslocamentos da teologia, mutações do cristianismo* (2001).

Address: Av. Dr. Cristiano Guimarães 2127, Planalto, 31720–300 Belo Horizonte.
E-mail: clarrrauri@hotmail.com

LEONARDO BOFF was born in 1938 and was for many years professor of systematic and ecumenical theology at the Franciscan Institute in Petrópolis-RJ. After his sentence to 'respectful silence' by the Vatican, he became professor of ethics and philosophy of religion at the State University of Rio de Janeiro. He is the author of over sixty books, many translated into English, including *Jesus Christ Liberator*; *Church: Charism and Power*; *Passion of Christ, Passion of the World*; *Trinity and Society*; *Good News to the Poor*. His more recent works deal with ecology and include *Ecology: Cry of the Earth, Cry of the Poor*.

Address: C.P. 92144, 27541 Petrópolis-RJ.

AGENOR BRIGHENTI is a priest and holds a doctorate in theological and religious sciences from the Catholic University of Louvain (1993) as well a licentiate in philosophy from the University of the South in Santa Catarina (UNISUL) (1975). He has been a specialist in social pastoral strategy with CELAM's Theological-Pastoral Institute for Latin America since 1980. He was pastoral co-ordinator for the diocese of Tubarão from 1981 to 1987 and academic director of ITEPAL-CELAM/Bogotá from 1994 to 1996. He currently teaches systematic theology at the Theological Institute of Santa

Catarina (ITESC), philosophy at UNISUL, and pastoral theology at the Pontifical University of Mexico (UPM).

Address: Caixa Postal 5041, 88040–970 Florianópolis-SC.
E-mail: agenorb@terra.com.br

BRENDA MARIBEL CARRANZA DÁVILA was born in Guatemala and has lived in Brazil for twelve years. Trained in philosophy, theology, psychology, and social sciences, she holds a Master's in sociology and a doctorate in social sciences from the State University of Campinas (UNICAMP). In Guatemala she played an active role in the 'War-Guerrilla Dialogue' as a representative of the Gautemalan Bishops Conference. In Brazil she has compiled reports for the CNBB, researched at the Centre for Religious Statistics and Social Investigations (CERIS), and been a tutor in university pastoral strategy at the Pontifical Catholic University of Campinas. She is on the editorial board of the journal *Novamerica* (which circulates throughout Latin America) and is a member of the publications committee of the textbook series *Tendências do Catolicismo Contemporâneo* published by CNBB/CERIS.

Address: Rua das Violetas 246, bl 13, apto.32, 13050–908 Campinas-SP.
E-mail: poveda@terra.com.br

MARIA CLARA LUCCHETTI BINGEMER lives in Rio de Janeiro. A laywoman, she is married with three grown-up children. She received a doctorate from the Gregorian in 1989 and is currently associate professor in the theology department at the Pontifical Catholic University in Rio and co-ordinator at the Loyola Centre of Faith and Culture at the same university. She is co-author with Ivone Gebara of *Mary: Mother of the Church, Mother of the Poor* (1993) and her other recent publications include *Deus trindade: a vida no coração do mundo* (2001, ed); *Violência e religião. Três religiões em confronto e dialogo: Cristianismo, Judaismo, Islamismo* (2001); *A identidade crítica. Identidade, vocação e missão dos leigos* (1998); *Em tudo amar e servir* (1990); *O segredo feminino do mistério* (1991).

Address: Rua Almirante Salgado 51, Laranjeiras, 22240–170 Rio de Janeiro-RJ.
E-mail: agape@rdc.puc-rio.br

AFONSO MARIA LIGORIO SOARES was born in Santo André-SP, where he lives with his wife, Raquel. He is assistant lecturer at the department of theology and sciences of religion at the Pontifical Catholic University of São Paulo and head of the department of dogmatic and pastoral theology at the Theology Institute of the diocese of Santo André-SP. He has been a member of the *Atabaque* – Black Theology and Culture – Group since 1990. He holds a degree in philosophy from PUC-PR and in theology from the Theological Institute of São Paulo (ITESP), a Master's in Dogmatic Theology from the Gregorian, and a doctorate in Sciences of Religion from the Methodist University of São Paulo (UMESP). His doctoral thesis was titled *Sincretismo e inculturação: pressupostos para uma aproximação teológico-pastoral às religiões afro-brasileiras buscados na epistemologia de Juan Luis Segundo* (2001). He is presently working on another doctoral thesis project in international relations at PUC-SP on the importance of inter-religious dialogue for a new platform of co-existence among the world religions.

Address: Av. Dr. Cesário Bastos n° 217, ap. 11, Jd. Bela Vista, 09040–330 Santo André-SP.
E-mail: sofona@uol.com.br

FRANCISCO WHITAKER FERREIRA has been a Christian militant since his young days as a member of Catholic Action in the 1950s, influenced by the ideas of Fr Lebret. Exiled as an activist from Brazil and subsequently from Chile, he involved himself in international organizations concerned with theThird World from Europe. On his return to Brazil he engaged in the church's social pastoral activity, 'accompanied' base communities, and became a recorder for the municipal chamber of the city of São Paulo. He soon left politics in order to devote more time to his activities as a member of the CNBB's Justice and Peace Commission, as which he takes part in the running of the World Social Forum, which he helped to devise.

Address: Rua Artur de Azevedo 1690, apto 401, 05404–004 São Paulo-SP.
E-mail: intercom@cidadanet.org.br

PEDRO CASALDÁLIGA was born in Catalonia and calls himself Brazilian by adoption. He is bishop of São Felix do Araguaia, having survived constant threat of assassination from military and right-wing sources over many years. Poet, writer of liturgies, missionary, defender of human rights, and Nobel Peace Prize candidate, he has worked resolutely for the poorest of the poor for thirty years. His works have been published in Catalan, French, German, Italian, Portuguese, Spanish, and other languages. Those translated into English include *Fire and Ashes to the Wind: A Spiritual Anthology* (1984); *In Pursuit of the Kingdom: Writings 1968–1988* (1990); *Spirituality of Liberation* (with J.-M. Vigil, 1994); *The Struggle is One: Voices and Visions of Liberation* (1994). His liturgies, including *Missa Quilombo* and *Missa da terra sem males*, are available on video and cassette.

Concilium Subscription Information

Issues published in 2002

February   2002/1: *The Many Voices of the Bible*
Edited by Seán Freyne and Ellen van Wolde

April   2002/2: *The Body and Religion*
Edited by Regina Ammicht-Quinn and Elsa Tamez

June   2002/3: *Brazil*
Edited by José Oscar Beozzo and Luiz Carlos Susin

October   2002/4: *Religious Education of Boys and Girls*
Edited by Werner Jeanrond and Lisa Sowle Cahill

December   2002/5: *The Rights of Women*
Edited by María Pilar Aquino Vargas and Elisabeth Schüssler Fiorenza

New subscribers: to receive *Concilium* 2002 (five issues) anywhere in the world, please copy this form, complete it in block capitals and send it with your payment to the address below.

Please enter my subscription for Concilium 2002

☐ Individual   **£25.00**/*US$50.00*   ☐ Institutional   **£35.00**/*US$75.00*

Issues are sent by air to the USA; please add £10/US$20 for airmail dispatch to all other countries (outside Europe).

☐ I enclose a cheque payable to SCM-Canterbury Press Ltd for £/$ ....

☐ Please charge my MasterCard/Visa   Expires ....

....................../.............................../................................./.............................

Signature ....

Name/Institution ....

Address ....

....

....

Telephone ....

Concilium   SCM Press   9–17 St Albans Place   London N1 0NX   England
Telephone (44) 20 7359 8033   Fax (44) 20 7359 0049
E-mail: scmpress@btinternet.com